PRAISE FOR
Love Your Enemies

"*If life is a struggle, this book is your friend. Its whispered truths,
like the first inklings of the dawn, bring both relief and
recognition. Return to it time and again; its good humor
and wise counsel are a balm for the soul.*"

—**Mark Epstein,** author of *The Trauma of Everyday Life*

"*If there are two beings in the whole world whom I trust with my
whole heart to give powerful, honest, kind, and deeply truthful
teachings that can free us from burning in the mental anguish that
is the 'new normal' in these anxious and fear-ridden times, it is
Tenzin Bob Thurman and Sharon Salzberg. Having known both of
them for many years, I can say that I am blessed that they are with
me on this desert island called Earth.*"

—**Krishna Das,** musician and author of *Chants of a Lifetime*

"*Brilliant!* Love Your Enemies *is possibly the most inspiring
and liberating meditation on love ever written.*"

—**Robert Holden, Ph.D.,** author of *Shift Happens!* and *Loveability*

LOVE YOUR ENEMIES

LOVE YOUR ENEMIES

HOW TO BREAK
THE ANGER HABIT AND
BE MUCH HAPPIER

SHARON SALZBERG
& ROBERT THURMAN

HAY HOUSE

Carlsbad, California • New York City • London • Sydney
Johannesburg • Vancouver • Hong Kong • New Delhi

First published and distributed in the United Kingdom by:
Hay House UK Ltd, Astley House, 33 Notting Hill Gate, London W11 3JQ
Tel: +44 (0)20 3675 2450; Fax: +44 (0)20 3675 2451
www.hayhouse.co.uk

Published and distributed in the United States of America by:
Hay House Inc., PO Box 5100, Carlsbad, CA 92018-5100
Tel: (1) 760 431 7695 or (800) 654 5126
Fax: (1) 760 431 6948 or (800) 650 5115
www.hayhouse.com

Published and distributed in Australia by:
Hay House Australia Ltd, 18/36 Ralph St, Alexandria NSW 2015
Tel: (61) 2 9669 4299; Fax: (61) 2 9669 4144
www.hayhouse.com.au

Published and distributed in the Republic of South Africa by:
Hay House SA (Pty) Ltd, PO Box 990, Witkoppen 2068
Tel/Fax: (27) 11 467 8904
www.hayhouse.co.za

Published and distributed in India by:
Hay House Publishers India, Muskaan Complex, Plot No.3, B-2,
Vasant Kunj, New Delhi 110 070
Tel: (91) 11 4176 1620; Fax: (91) 11 4176 1630
www.hayhouse.co.in

Distributed in Canada by:
Raincoast, 9050 Shaughnessy St, Vancouver BC V6P 6E5
Tel: (1) 604 323 7100; Fax: (1) 604 323 2600

Copyright © 2013 by Sharon Salzberg and Robert Thurman

The moral rights of the authors have been asserted.

Cover design: Shelley Noble • *Interior design:* Celia Fuller-Vels

The information given in this book should not be treated as a substitute for professional medical advice; always consult a medical practitioner. Any use of information in this book is at the reader's discretion and risk. Neither the authors nor the publisher can be held responsible for any loss, claim or damage arising out of the use, or misuse, of the suggestions made, the failure to take medical advice or for any material on third party websites.

A catalogue record for this book is available from the British Library.

ISBN: 978-1-84850-306-9

Printed and bound in Great Britain by TJ International Ltd, Padstow, Cornwall.

For all those who express their strength through compassion instead of anger, whether within themselves, their families, their communities, or their nations. May love and kindness prevail.

SHARON SALZBERG

To all sensitive beings of all kinds,
may they come through the present crises and flourish,
and especially
TO ALL WOMEN,
the Cool Heroines of our world,
full and free individuals, heroic warriors, true friends, mothers,
wives, daughters, whose labor—all kinds, love, intelligence,
creativity, courage, tolerance, kindness, diplomacy, self-sacrifice,
good humor, and ever deeper and broader vision—through the
millennia and every day and night, save families, their sisters,
unruly males, parents, partners, children, nonhuman animals,
whole communities, and the very planet, from misery and self-
destruction! May this little book contribute in some small way to
these Great Souls' receiving the honor, respect, and authority they so
richly deserve and we all so urgently need them to have!

TENZIN ROBERT THURMAN

Contents

How to Use This Book

L ove Your Enemies is a practical guide to finding freedom from our enemies, through the powerful allies of wisdom, tolerance, and love. Specifically, we offer tools to conquer four kinds of enemies we encounter in life—these four developed from the ancient Tibetan mind-transformation teachings:

- **The outer enemy:** the people and institutions that harass, disturb, or harm us in some way, as well as situations that frustrate us
- **The inner enemy:** anger, hatred, fear, and other destructive impulses
- **The secret enemy:** self-obsession and self-preoccupation, which isolate us from other people, leaving us frustrated and alone
- **The super-secret enemy:** deep-seated self-loathing that keeps us from finding inner freedom and true happiness

We present the enemies in this order in the book, progressing from outer enemies inward, since the process of finding freedom through overcoming our anger, fear, and self-preoccupation generally proceeds more or less in this order. But life is ever-changing and unpredictable, and we are well aware that we do not always meet our enemies in such an orderly fashion. So we encourage you to start where you are. Perhaps you are so hard on yourself that you cannot even start to face your enemies because the whole enterprise seems hopeless. You might first turn to the Appendix and practice the lovingkindness meditation to develop self-compassion before diving in. Or you might skip ahead and read Chapter 4 on the super-secret enemy for a sense of the boundless joy and inner freedom that lies ahead. Perhaps what is causing you anguish at the moment is the habitual anger you harbor; you could begin with Chapter 2 on vanquishing the inner enemy.

Regardless of which enemies we are facing, the method of overcoming them is the same. First, using critical wisdom, we clearly identify the enemy—not quite as simple as it sounds—and then we engage mindfulness to experience fully how it operates. Next, we move toward dismantling our adversarial relationship with the enemy by learning to tolerate it and then by developing compassion for it, even as we take decisive action to root it out. Finally, freed of our enemies, we can relax in the bliss of true happiness and the joy of living harmoniously with others. Working with our enemies is both an inner and an outer process.

Freeing ourselves is not easy. It takes intelligence, courage, and persistence to break away from habitual ways of looking at the world and to respond in a different and more productive manner. On one level, dealing effectively with our enemies calls for restraint—not lashing out in rage or retaliation, not indulging a desire for revenge. On another level, it involves actively engaging with the world so that instead of expressing our anger and fear in destructive ways, we take constructive action from a place of kindness toward others and ourselves.

Ultimately we come to understand that there is no "us" and "them," no separation between self and other, and therefore, no enemy. Victory over our enemies is a deep realization of our interdependence.

For years, we have been teaching a weekend workshop on coming to terms with one's enemies. This book is an outgrowth of that workshop. We have designed it as a workbook to help you identify your enemies and transform your relationship to them.

In the spiritual context, "love" means to wish for the happiness of someone, and this is what we're encouraging you to do in regard to your enemies. The command to love everyone, including those that harm you—as put forth by many great spiritual teachers, such as Buddha and Jesus—has often been viewed as undesirable or even impossible. However, it is worth considering that it is in fact eminently possible and practical to wish true happiness for your enemy, for this is the only way to be free of the torment brought on by them. The benefit of this love is twofold. If it brings happiness to an enemy, this enemy is much less likely to cause harm or frustration to those around him. However, if this viewpoint of love has no immediate effect on your enemy, the mere act of loving brings with it an inner peace.

In this book, we draw upon many spiritual traditions, as well as modern psychology, to present tools that are useful for anyone of any faith—or for the skeptic—to help in this quest of changing your relationship to your enemies and learning to live a life guided by wisdom, tolerance, compassion, and love. We hope you will find in these teachings and exercises something you can experiment with. Think of it as a grand experiment in seeing yourself differently, seeing others differently, and coming to a different understanding of genuine strength and true happiness.

Before Bob became a college professor and author, he lived in India as the first Westerner to be ordained a Tibetan Buddhist monk. Sharon studied meditation in India and Burma with teachers in the Theravada tradition, and then returned to America to co-found a Buddhist retreat center in central Massachusetts.

When we teach together, we alternate teachings and stories, exercises and meditations, just as we have done in these pages.

Sharon's stories, teachings, and examples, drawn from her own life experience and that of her students, will appear in type that looks like this.

Bob's teachings, drawing on the Buddhist canon and his personal experiences, will appear in type that looks like this.

SHARON SALZBERG

TENZIN ROBERT THURMAN

NEW YORK, 2013

Introduction

SHARON SALZBERG

We all want to be happy, but there is such confusion about where genuine happiness is to be found. All around us we see people in conflict, acting out of an Us-versus-Them mentality. This feeling of separation and alienation leads us to think that the way to happiness must lie in triumphing over others or repressing parts of ourselves. We often end up seeing others as enemies; and when things don't go our way, we become enemies to ourselves.

Our personal and collective conditioning can lead us to think of strength as something quite different from kindness and compassion. Therefore, unless we are making an enemy of some person or situation, we may feel as if we are giving in or giving up, acting in a way that is foolish or weak or self-destructive. I believe this sense of enmity and separation, this sense of division from others and within ourselves, is at the heart of our confusion about where true happiness lies.

The premise of this book is that we all have enemies, even though—spoiler alert—Bob will throw you a curveball in that regard (see page xix). But then, inspired by Buddhist teachings, we will lead you on a journey through the four kinds of enemies we encounter: outer enemies, inner enemies, secret enemies, and super-secret enemies. Outer enemies are the people who harass or annoy us, as well as life situations that frustrate or confound us. Inner enemies are the habits of our reactive mind—particularly anger and hatred—that enslave us to and play havoc with our lives. Deeper still we find our secret enemy, the self-absorption that cuts us off from others and from our own loving nature. And finally, there is the super-secret enemy, the deeply entrenched sense of self-loathing that keeps us from realizing our kinship with all beings. The teachings and meditations in this book help us to draw on our own innate wisdom and compassion in order to transform our relationship with our enemies, both inner and outer.

When most of us hear the word *enemies,* we probably think immediately of all the people who have actually hurt or harmed us. But there are also tricky adversaries that we all have to contend with—our own inner enemies. Together, in this guide, we will uncover the subtleties of working with these enemies, for this is where real victory lies.

When we encounter an enemy, whether outer or inner, we tend to go around and around in the same kind of habitual thinking that has failed to resolve the situation in the past—thinking that leaves us feeling frustrated and angry and unfulfilled. It is an act of audacity to step out of these familiar but flawed ways of dealing with our enemies and seek another, better way. It takes courage to be willing to try approaches that shift the enemy dynamic of Us-versus-Them. The social psychologist Jonathan Haidt refers to the strategy of shifting our rigid, entrenched, same-old thinking as stepping outside our "moral matrix." When we refuse to return anger with anger, when we reject the belief that revenge is our only option, we step out of our moral matrix into a limitless world of enlightened choice.

Our society tends to dismiss kindness as a minor virtue, rather than the tremendous force it can truly be. Although the Dalai Lama is revered the world over as the embodiment of kindness and compassion, his refusal to see the Chinese who have overrun Tibet as enemies is incomprehensible to many people. But overcoming our enemies requires being able to step away from our assumptions and regard kindness and compassion as the strengths they really are. Among the practices we introduce in the book is one of this most powerful for dissolving enmity: lovingkindness meditation.

"Lovingkindness" is a translation of the word *metta*, from Pali, the language of the original Buddhist texts. *Metta* has also been translated as "love" and "friendship." Lovingkindness is a deep knowing that every individual's life is inextricably interwoven with all life and that, because of that connection, we need to take care of one another—not out of sloppy sentimentality or a sense of obligation, but out of wisdom that recognizes that when we care for others, we are really caring for ourselves.

Lovingkindness isn't just an abstract ideal; it's a hands-on, practical path to realizing a transformed life. As a meditation method, it opens our awareness so that we pay attention to ourselves and others in a different way. Instead of being distracted and fragmented, we learn to gather our attention and become centered. Instead of fixating only on what is wrong with us and feeling defeated by it, we learn to see the good within ourselves as well. And instead of reflexively categorizing people as bad and dismissing them, we pause to appreciate that, just like us, they want to be happy, too.

True happiness, as the Buddha saw it, is a form of resilience, an inner resource that allows us to care about ourselves and others without feeling depleted or overcome by whatever suffering we encounter. The perspectives and practices we describe in this book are ways of getting in touch with that resiliency and allowing it to guide us in all our relationships. Including our enemies in this process of transformation may seem impossible at first, but ultimately we come to realize that it is not only practical but liberating.

Introduction

TENZIN ROBERT THURMAN

Let's get one thing straight: *ultimately, we have no enemies.* We think of an enemy as someone—or something—that blocks our happiness. But no other being can block our happiness; true happiness comes from within. Therefore, ultimately, we have no enemies.

Right about now I can hear you saying, "What gives? Here's a whole book about working with our enemies and turning them into friends that starts out by telling me I have no enemies! That can't be right. I *know* I have enemies. Just yesterday I found out my co-worker is lobbying for the promotion I deserve. And what about my neighbors who blast music late into the night, keeping me awake? Or certain members of my family, who made my life miserable growing up? And what about the world today, with so many warring factions and everybody blowing each other up? No enemies? No way!"

In one sense you are right. Relatively speaking, we do have enemies. We perceive people and situations that harm us in some way as enemies. They harm what we identify as "myself," which, as we'll see, is part of the problem. While we perceive these outer enemies as being intent on harming us as much as possible, what is really under attack is our self-addiction, our sense of being a fixed, unchanging self, separate from other selves. So our more important enemy is the inner enemy, including the anger, hatred, and emotional turmoil that arise when our precious sense of self is threatened.

And our enemies do not stop there. Deeper still is our secret enemy—our fixed-identity habit or instinct, allied with our tenacious, unrelenting self-preoccupation, which shuts us off from reality and from loving interaction with others. And finally, there is our super-secret enemy—super-secret because it is hidden even from ourselves. This enemy is our collective shadow side—a primal, habitual sense of unworthiness we feel as human beings that is the last enemy standing in the way of real happiness and freedom.

Jesus commanded us to love our enemies, to turn the other cheek when we are harmed, to give our coat when asked for our shirt, to go the extra mile. The Buddha taught the same message, that only love can conquer hate, and he also showed us how to get started toward loving our enemies by using the energies coming from our outer enemy to overcome the inner enemy, using our insight into our inner enemy to overcome the secret enemy, and our freedom from the secret enemy to overcome the super-secret enemy. Working with our enemies in this way, we can come to love all our enemies, inner and outer.

Love wishes the real happiness of the beloved. It is a partner to compassion, which wishes the beloved not to suffer. If you think about it, it is highly rational to love our enemies, with *love* defined as wanting them to be really happy. They are only our enemies because they think of us as preventing their happiness. If they become really happy without having to get us out of their way, then they will not bother being our enemies anymore. The more happiness they feel, they might actually come to love us—or at least leave us alone.

We might reasonably question whether loving our enemies is safe. Won't they just take advantage of us, or even destroy us? Loving our enemies doesn't mean encouraging other people to harm us, however. Not only would we suffer then, but neither does harming us bring our enemies real happiness. The false happiness they get from tormenting us does not satisfy them and only leads to further unhappiness for them in the future or in future lives.

The kind of happiness we associate with destroying our enemies is false happiness because it is temporary. It arises circumstantially, when we receive momentary relief from stress through some external or internal shift. But when circumstances change, as they invariably do, this false happiness vanishes. And when it does, we suffer. The Buddha called this feeling "the suffering of change."

So false happiness doesn't last, but real happiness is reliable. It doesn't depend on circumstances but arises from a direct experiencing of reality—from awareness of what is happening here and now. We know real happiness intuitively: it is beyond words. Indeed, our words and thoughts constantly distract us from what we intuit. Our minds then create a distorted view of reality that we take to be true.

If we somehow intuit that we are deluded about what is real—we "get" that we have traded reality for fantasy—we might assume that all we need to do is turn off our thinking and we will automatically experience reality. But it's not that easy. Our long-ingrained patterns of delusion alienate us too radically from our intuitive ability to discern the truth. So we need to use our minds skillfully to unravel our entrapment in words and ideas, carefully to strip away the screen that covers deeper, inexpressible, inconceivable reality, while controlling the fear that makes us resist such revelation.

The Buddha's message is that we can awaken from wrong thinking to a more realistic way of living. And our enemies can be our best teachers. If there weren't people trying to harm us or keep us from getting what we want, how would we learn patience and tolerance and forgiveness?

It is a bit hard to make sense of the Buddha's view of our heroic potential to adopt a new normal of extreme happiness and natural heroism in overcoming our instinctive tendency to react angrily toward enemies. It is important to take into account one of the Buddha's most important scientific—not at all religious, in the sense of "mystical"—discoveries, what he experienced as the biological reality of sentient life. The theory of karma, which can be translated simplistically as "action," was taught by Buddha—millennia before Charles Darwin—to be a causal process of individual sentient evolution, which can be positive or negative, up or down in form and quality of life, through which all sentient beings are genetically related, since each of them has been reborn again and again in every single possible life-form, from the beginningless past. He realized that he himself had been a monkey, a lion, a turtle, a bacteria, a female, a male, a demon, a deity, etc., innumerable times, and so had everybody else. The present human life-form was thus seen as a huge evolutionary achievement of an amazingly complex, intelligent, and compassionate being; though there is no guarantee one will always be reborn human. The Buddha described what he saw as a Darwinian-ish ocean of life forms, in which an individual's "mental" or "spiritual" "gene," i.e. seed shaped by previous evolutionary experience and action, in turn shaping the future, is just as influential as the physical genes of parents in determining the form of a particular life.

That is, the modern materialist biologist considers the individual to be a product of random mutations of insentient physical genetic patterns, her mind to be an illusion produced by signals in a physical brain, and her life beginning only at birth and ending at death. Such a person is a mechanical creature with no long-term individual purpose, "hard-wired" to act and react in such a way as to enhance the future of his physical genes. Therefore, if an enemy threatens that gene enhancement, the machine individual is programmed to react with adrenaline- and cortisol-fuelled violence to destroy that enemy. No other course of action can make sense. The Buddha and his successor "mind scientists," on the contrary, see the individual as coming from a long evolutionary process in which the results of her mental and physical ethical actions are encoded in a mental gene (*chittagotra*) which shapes her present life, and so she has a very strong evolutionary motive to act in such a way that her individual quality and form of life is enhanced and further evolved as she continues in future lives, perhaps even into an endless future. Negative evolutionary regress, according to Buddha's presentation, is caused by selfish actions of mind and speech as well as body, and positive evolutionary progress is caused by altruistic actions. Anger and hatred as violent mental actions, and violent verbal and physical actions driven by them, thus drive an individual to evolve downward to ever lower forms of life, such as nonhuman animals, and even worse. And patience and love as gentle actions and motivators of gentle verbal and physical actions cause the individual's evolutionary progress toward ever better forms of life.

In this book, I will not be going into the intricate details of the Buddha's biological theory of karma, but I do invoke the individual evolutionary horizon within which our struggle to overcome anger and hatred is motivated by the realistic personal concerns of enlightened self-interest. I refer now and then to karma as "evolutionary action," and explain how the teachings of methods of overcoming anger make sense and seem less extreme when understood as referring to causes and effects over a continuum of lives, rather than only in the single life that materialists will allow a sentient being to have. Those readers who themselves have consciously chosen the materialist worldview as preferable to any sort of "religious view" of former and/or future lives, can still use these methods to obtain results of improvement of form and quality of life within this one life. Religious persons who are concerned for their future lives can also use these methods within their particular religious worldview, as they are mind-science-derived methods that can enhance our skill in dealing with our emotional and social lives, without requiring us to change our belief systems.

Whatever our scientific worldview, if we strive to go after our outer enemies in a more skillful way, we will soon come to see that our most important enemy is the inner one. The Dalai Lama's refusal to make the Chinese who have occupied Tibet into an enemy inspires us to see how conquering the inner enemy of anger can give us the ability to work with the people we think are harming us in such a way that we end up with the inner victory of real happiness, while wishing the best even for those enemies.

The notion of anger as our protector is the biggest obstacle to developing effective courage, or freedom from fear. Can you imagine what life would be like if you lived without unreasonable fear? You could even go through the screening line at the airport without being afraid the TSA would haul you aside because you forgot and packed that big bottle of fancy French shampoo in your carry-on.

Since enemies engage our energies of anger and fear, our main weapons against them are wisdom, tolerance, compassion, and love. Wisdom helps us become fearless by understanding the natural safety of truly deep reality. Tolerance helps us to not lose our wisdom in anger and hatred. Compassion expands our wisdom, forestalling the urge to create enemies. And love arises from the inner bliss of relief from anger and delusion—and overflows to embrace all beings everywhere. Our enemies gradually cease to perceive us as a threat—sometimes all too gradually—and their hostility lessens. In this way, we achieve lasting victory over our enemies.

WE ARE
THE TRAFFIC

Once I was on a train going down the Hudson Valley to New York City and found myself sitting between a woman engaged in a rather loud conversation on her cellphone and a man growing increasingly agitated by the volume of her call. As the ride went on, accompanied by the steady sound of her voice and the minute details of her plans, he wiggled, grunted, muttered, and finally exploded. "You're making too much noise!" he yelled at the top of his lungs. I looked over at him and thought, *Well, so are you!*

When we are caught in gridlock and freak out about the traffic, we forget that we, too, are the traffic. We may be part of the problem as well as, potentially, part of the solution. Working with our antagonists begins with a willingness to step into new terrain and explore the zone between those we care about and draw toward us, and those we wall off and reject. The philosopher Peter Singer calls this process "expanding the moral circle" of those about whom we are concerned.

Although altruism began as a biological drive to protect our own, he explained, it evolved into a choice to care for others. Our knee-jerk reaction may be to drown out someone else's noise by shouting back or to return belligerence with unkindness, but ultimately this is an exhausting, vicious circle of conflict.

Designating someone as the enemy fixes that person in an immutable identity. When we categorize others as bad (or good, or right or wrong), it enables us to feel secure. We know just where we—and they—stand. Or so we think. But life is more complex than that. My friend Brett, who once drove for a limo company, describes being enraged one day at the behavior of other drivers. Then he realized that he himself, at one point or another, had committed the same transgressions he was so upset about.

Relating to others as if they're in a category completely apart from us objectifies them, creating tensions that invariably escalate into conflict. It does not allow for easy connection and can leave us quite lonely. In the situation with the cellphone user on the train, a more fruitful approach to dealing with the perceived enemy might be to change seats, if possible, or to politely ask the caller to lower her voice. An alternative would be to not respond at all in the moment but to later take positive action, such as lobbying against cellphone use on public transportation or advocating for quiet cars on commuter lines. Instead of lashing out at people who offend us, we could work instead to turn the situation into an opportunity to benefit all involved.

Brett tells a story about his first silent meditation retreat ten years ago. It was the annual lovingkindness retreat I teach at the Insight Meditation Society, a center I co-founded in Barre, Massachusetts. One evening several days into the retreat, he was resting in his room after dinner, before going into the meditation hall for the evening sitting. He vividly recalls what happened next:

> My room was located right above the phone booth in the basement. I was lying on my bed, feeling a warm current of love flowing through me, when suddenly I heard a loud, forceful voice in the basement below. I couldn't make out what was being said, but I could tell it was a man yelling. My mind immediately went from well-wishing to thinking, *How dare he!* I was incensed enough to get up and head downstairs to tell this guy how wrong he was for speaking so loudly in our tranquil sanctuary. I opened the basement door and looked across the floor to the phone booth,

where I could just see the top of the offender's head. When I got close enough to actually make out what he was saying, I heard him shout, in obvious frustration, "But Dad, we paid three thousand dollars for your hearing aid; you really ought to be using it!" At that moment, all the adrenaline in my system melted back into a field of lovingkindness, and I smiled and went back to my room.

There is nothing weak or defeatist about not confronting our enemies directly and aggressively. Rather, it is a completely different way of relating to others that allows us to avoid being trapped in the role of victim or aggressor. We are so conditioned to relating to others in adversarial terms that we seldom think of how futile that is as an everyday code of conduct. As Brett discovered, we can learn a lot about what is really going on in the pause between feeling angry and taking action.

CHAPTER 1

Victory over
the Outer Enemy

We meet the outer enemy when we have been harmed. In everyday life, all sorts of harm can come to us. We—and our loved ones—may be insulted or abused, robbed or beaten, bullied or tormented, tortured or even killed. Our property may be taken, damaged, or destroyed. The people who commit such acts fit neatly into the normal definition of an enemy: a person who hates another and wishes or tries to injure him or her. We feel perfectly justified in labeling such perpetrators our enemies and treating them accordingly.

Other people, too, may be abused or harmed, and if we identify with them, we consider the people who harm them our enemies as well. We find no end of enemies in books and movies and TV shows, where the bad guys are doing bad things to the good guys. Naturally we identify with the good guys, and we wait in suspense for them to catch the bad guys and save the day.

Other outer enemies that cause us much pain are the many things we see going wrong in the world and the people we perceive as responsible for them: economic inequity that favors the super-rich over everyone else, industries that pollute our waterways and turn empty lots into Superfund sites, politicians who play fast and loose with our social entitlements and constitutional rights, well-financed interest groups that push their narrow agendas to the forefront. Everywhere we look, we can find some group antagonizing another group.

We need look no farther than our neighborhood or the local school to find enemies galore. Teenaged shooters and terrorists grab today's headlines, but an even more insidious and widespread problem is bullying, which has reached epidemic proportions. Race, creed, nationality, social class, gender orientation—even a stutter or the "wrong" clothes can invite abuse and attacks, with sometimes fatal consequences.

We only have to open a newspaper or turn on the TV to be confronted with enemies across the world. When we see one country attacking another or turning on its own people, we feel deeply upset by the carnage and want to see the aggressors defeated. When our own country is the aggressor—I think of the "shock-and-awe" bombing of Baghdad—we are torn between our desire to vanquish the bad guys and our sadness and guilt over the human suffering that results from resorting to violence.

We try to make ourselves invulnerable to harm, but merely shielding ourselves or running away from it is only a temporary fix. Sooner or later, harm will find us. The only sure way to make ourselves invulnerable is to change our view of enemies and learn to see every instance of harm as an opportunity—as something we can use to benefit ourselves and others. From this perspective, how could we possibly grow in strength and burnish the shining armor of patience *without* having someone or something attempt to harm us, to give us a chance to learn to restrain our reactions of irritation, victimization, anger, and fear? We need enemies for this. We should be grateful for our enemies, the Dalai Lama has said, for they teach us patience, courage, and determination, and help us develop a tranquil mind.

To deal effectively with our enemies, we have to overcome our hatred and fear of those who harm us, intend to harm us, have harmed us in the past, or might harm us in the future. That's a tall order for most of us, at least at first. Coming to terms with our enemies is best taken slowly, in incremental steps.

Right away, let me assure you that we are not suggesting you simply lie down and let whoever wants to harm you take a shot. That would be masochistic, serving no one. To deal with our enemies, we can start by doing everything possible to avoid the people who wish us harm, in order to keep them from being in a position to carry out their hurtful plans. If we can't avoid them, however, we do then need to defend ourselves. But between avoidance and defensiveness lies a middle way. The best strategy of all is to act preemptively, skillfully, and before we are angry, and not allow our enemies the opportunity to harm us.

In all these strategies, we are looking on the person as a potential danger, not unlike a truck coming toward us on the highway. We anticipate the truck's path and take precautions to avoid it. But we don't hate the truck; we don't make an enemy of it. We just take care to stay safely on our side of the road.

Granted, it's hard not to hate our enemies. When we're hurt, we automatically feel victimized and respond with anger, hatred, or fear. So the question, at least with our outer enemies, is how can we conquer them without returning fire with fire? How do we avoid reacting when we feel that we're under attack? It takes a clear understanding of the situation to avoid reacting, to exercise physical and verbal restraint. So to assist us in dealing with our enemies, we need the powerful intelligence of critical wisdom—as its penetrating analysis of the real situation can free us from losing ourselves in clumsy gut reactions.

BULLYING

Bullying is on the rise, manifesting in behaviors that range from spreading gossip to shunning to physical violence. The bully's many tools include derisive laughter, vicious mocking, staring, and giving someone the silent treatment. While definitive statistics on bullying vary, there is no question that a large percentage of students experience bullying of one kind or another during their lifetime—according to one source, up to 77 percent of students face it![1]

In the schoolyard, at the workplace, on the Web, even at the hands of government agencies and religious organizations, bullying is becoming a way of life. Bullying may be directed toward particular victims on the grounds of race, religion, sex, or ability, or it may flare up in isolated acts of hostility and cruelty.

Bullying is the deep end of the Us-versus-Them swimming pool, where run-of-the-mill unkindness blossoms into a hostile assault on the victim's body or character. Often born of the bully's deep insecurity, bullying operates through exclusion and attack. Rather than admit their own weakness, bullies control their anxiety by displacing it, striking out at easy targets. Individuals and groups who perceive themselves as victims tend to make the most suitable targets for bullying. In a staggering majority of these incidents, bystanders or the bully's friends join in teasing the victim or egging on the bully.

Social isolation is a more subtle but no less painful form of bullying. I saw this close up in the experience of a Euro-American friend's young daughter who was adopted from China. On the girl's very first day at a progressive urban school, the children in her class were asked to describe one way in which they physically resembled their

1   Bullying Statistics: http://www.bullyingstatistics.org/content/bullying-statistics.html

mother or father. She came home sobbing. "I was the only one who had nothing to say," she said.

I can remember feeling the same way as a child, when my father was a patient in a psychiatric hospital. In class, the teachers would ask us to say what our fathers did for a living, and I did not know what to say. Each time something like that happened, my sense of isolation and shame deepened.

Systems can bully as much as individuals. Social structures promote bullying through stereotyping, through class hierarchy, or most insidiously, through various forms of thought control. Unfortunately, it is not just in cults and totalitarian regimes that people are deliberately fed misinformation and told not to think what they are naturally thinking. In his pioneering work of the 1950s, the social scientist Gregory Bateson identified the destructive force of mixed messages like these.

When we perceive a subtext beneath the party line, the cognitive dissonance can be crazy-making. This is a common, if often unconscious, ploy in families in which the truth dare not be spoken. Think of the parent who is beating a child while telling her it is for her own good. Or the mother who acts as if everything is peachy at home, while her children see clearly that her cheery smile masks enormous suffering. Addiction recovery programs refer to these secret shames as the elephant in the living room, the huge, obvious problems that everyone pretends aren't there.

Bullying someone into silence or humiliating them or undermining their sense of reality is a sure way to create an enemy. Bringing the truth into the open gives us our power back, but confronting a bully head-on can be dangerous. When I was working with abused women in a domestic violence shelter, the standard advice to the women was to "go to school when he's not looking" and acquire skills that would give them economic freedom.

Psychological disengagement from a bully is more important than attempting to make him see the light. Taking self-respect back from an abuser is an inside job that requires neither his knowledge nor his permission.

It takes a lot of courage to stand up for ourselves, with many voices telling us to do the opposite—to avoid, hide, or deny what's happening. I know a woman whose father-in-law is a serious alcoholic, while her mother-in-law is one of those people who's too polite to talk about it. Recently, when this woman and her husband visited her in-laws, her father-in-law couldn't get out of bed for dinner. When she asked if he was drinking again, her mother-in-law replied, "Not to speak of."

This is how we can be bullied into silence by those we love, not to mention by society at large. A hallmark of bullying is humiliation. It is humiliating to have our subjective reality questioned or invalidated. "Here, take the feel-good-about-life pill," we're told, like the characters in Aldous Huxley's novel *Brave New World*, when in reality, the situation is causing great misery or hardship.

Unsure what to believe, we feel ashamed and worthless, caught in a vicious circle of self-abnegation that feeds on the gruel of false information. Acknowledging that our feelings are authentic can be extremely healing. The truth gives us back our power and with it our effectiveness in the world.

Let's be clear: critical wisdom is fierce—unflinching, uncompromising, even ferocious—yet at the same time, subtle and tender. In Buddhist imagery, critical wisdom is represented by the sword of Manjushri, a divine bodhisattva (enlightenment hero) whose name means "gentle glory." In Tibetan icons, Manjushri's sword is razor-sharp, with a golden handle and a blue steel blade with fire blazing from its tip. This sharp sword represents critical, analytical intelligence. Critical wisdom carried to the furthest level can also be represented by a ferocious emanation of Manjushri, Vajrabhairava ("Diamond Terrifier") or Yamantaka ("Death-Exterminator"), an exquisite symbolic embodiment of immortal life as the "death of Death!" (We will invoke Yamantaka to help us overcome the secret enemy in Chapter 3.) Also, to show the breadth of critical wisdom and its softer side, it is also represented by the beautiful goddess Prajñaparamita, or "Transcendent Wisdom." Known as the Mother of all Buddhas—because transcendent wisdom gives birth to enlightenment—she holds in her many hands not just weapons (a bow and arrow, and a sword and a scepter) but also a book and a lotus flower.

"Why the ferocity of critical wisdom?" you might ask. "Aren't we trying to not respond to the enemy with hostility?" True. But insight must be fierce to overcome fear, anger, fury, hate, vengeance, malice—all the ingredients that go into making an enemy, and they all come from our misunderstanding of the reality of our situation. So critical wisdom must be fierce in its laserlike penetrating concentration to enable us to see through our confusion.

And what is the reality of our situation? In other words, what's the worst that can happen? What's the gravest danger our enemy can inflict on us? Okay, we must face that we can be insulted, injured, or even killed by enemies. We are right to be afraid of those outcomes. Such fear is healthy; it energizes us to avoid such enemies. But we can avoid them or even defend ourselves against them much more skillfully if we master our fear and anger and keep our cool, like a martial artist. One way we can do that is to rehearse the various outcomes, imagining even the worst ones. Surprisingly, it can help to think carefully about each outcome.

We tend to get angry when someone insults us, for example. But how bad can any insult be? Will any name we are called cause us lasting harm? Can't we just laugh it off, especially since most insults are exaggerations in the first place? We're seldom as bad as the enemy makes us out to be. And we need not worry about the effect of the insult on others who overhear it, as usually the insulter is the one who looks bad. How about the wisdom of the child's slogan, "Sticks and stones will break my bones, but words will never hurt me!"

And what about the sticks and stones, even physical kinds of harm? Of course we must protect ourselves, but if we do get hurt, what good does it do us to get angry on top of suffering the hurt? The Dalai Lama tells a story about a servant he had in Tibet, who tried to fix an old car that had belonged to the previous Dalai Lama. While working on the old car, the mechanic would occasionally skin his knuckles. Losing his temper, he would bang his head repeatedly on the underside of the car. Trying to calm him down, the Dalai Lama would get him to see the humor of it, telling him, "The car doesn't feel anything!"

Anger often makes us hurt ourselves more than any enemy. If an enemy hurts us, that is bad enough; we should avoid hurting ourselves by overanticipating the hurt and being paralyzed by fear, unable to face the enemy with all our faculties at their best.

But let's be really radical, rise to the occasion, and imagine even the ultimate harm: the enemy could kill us. Do we ever think about dying? It could happen at any time, after all, just by accident, without any enemy. We probably live mostly in denial of that fact, but it may be that our subliminal yet ever-present fear of death prevents us from feeling fully alive. What does death mean to us? What do you think happens to you at death? Maybe you have a strong sense of an afterlife and think that after death you will ascend to heaven, by the blessing of Jesus, Buddha, or some other God or angel (though hellish prospects might scare you, you'll have found help or a sure way to avoid the danger). Or maybe you're a secularist and your sense of an afterlife is to think that after death you will simply disappear—become an unconscious nothing forever after. Either way, again, though it might happen, there's no point to overanticipating it while alive and letting the enemy hold your anticipation over you.

Anyway, what we really fear is not death but dying—a transition that we anticipate could be deeply painful. Of course our instinct is to save our life at any cost, but that instinct is reinforced to our greater endangerment by our unexamined notions of what death is. Paralyzed by fear or driven mad with anger, it's just so much harder to save or enhance our life. We either become unable to respond at all, becoming a helpless victim, or we lash out ineffectively, fail to stop the enemy, and sometimes provoke an even worse reaction. So if we can free ourselves from the excessive fear of the unrealistic outcomes that we anticipate, we improve our chances of avoiding those very outcomes. Mark Twain famously said he had "known a great many troubles, but most of them never happened."

We fear pain much more than death, when we face it clearly. Mercifully, most of us will not be forced to endure physical torture at the hands of an enemy. But imagining how we might handle it can be instructive in strengthening our resilience. The most practical method for dealing with pain would be *restraint*—not being angry with either our victimhood or our tormentors, since such reactivity only makes the pain worse and arouses the tormentor to greater viciousness. Hatred does not help us alleviate our pain even in the slightest. Tibetan monks who were imprisoned under harrowing conditions often attribute their survival to not getting caught up in anger toward their guards. If, instead of anger, we conceive that every single pain our torturers are dishing out now will make us better able to deal with any future pain, then bearing it will seem like an achievement. Further, if we have a commonsense understanding of the observable truth that "What comes around, goes around!"—or, even better, if we know of the law of evolutionary, biological causality that is called "karma"—we might be able to consider that every pain our enemies inflict on us is the very pain they themselves will suffer in the future—or future existence—not to mention the guilt they suffer subliminally even at the moment. With this view, we might even be able to summon up sympathy for our torturers. Jesus's plea from the cross, "Father, forgive them, for they know not what they do!" might echo in our ears.

Much of the harm we suffer at the hands of our enemies is emotional. But here, too, we can expand the range of the "no pain, no gain!" motto, and try to use any sort of suffering inflicted on us to strengthen our ability to not waste energy hating those who wrong us. If we can learn to not be angry with them, we will be arming ourselves with the greatest possible protection: *tolerance*. With the shield of tolerance, we become stronger and more resilient, better able to deal with efforts by our enemies to inflict whatever kind of pain.

The basic obstacle, however, to overcoming our anger toward our enemies is our thought that, unless we have the strength of anger, they will trample us. Anger, to this way of thinking, is protective. It gives strength to resist, and without it we are weak. But if we look at our experience more carefully, we can catch anger in the act of tricking us, making us feel stronger by heating us up, but actually weakening us by impairing our judgment and causing us to exert our energy all at once in unsustainable bursts. According to neuroscientific studies, it also harms our health by releasing noxious chemicals such as cortisol into our bloodstream, which damage our circulatory system.

Overcoming our enmity toward others does not mean surrendering to them. On the contrary, when threatened, we can defend ourselves more effectively if we deal with aggression without hatred or anger. The martial arts teach us that to gain the power to defeat our opponents, we must transcend anger. As any martial artist will tell you, anger throws you off balance and exhausts you too quickly, making you more vulnerable to your enemy's attack. Excessive fear can do the same thing.

Being afraid when we are under attack is natural. But we can handle the situation much more competently if the fear we are feeling is the good kind of fear—the cautionary fear that warns us of legitimate threats to our safety and prompts a constructive reaction—and not the paranoid, paralyzing fear that prevents us from acting with good judgment and unflagging energy.

CRUSHING THE COMPETITION

Competition today is tantamount to a blood sport—and not just on the playing field or in the ring. The psychoanalytic theorist Karen Horney introduced the concept of hypercompetitiveness as a neurotic personality trait almost 70 years ago. She characterized the hypercompetitive coping strategy as "moving against people" (in contrast to moving toward or away from people). Her observations are now all too evident in our culture. Extreme Us-versus-Them behavior has created a lonely world. There is always some new adversary to move against, so we get locked into a vicious circle of measuring our strength by disparaging others. I remember watching the ice dancing competition at the Winter Olympics one year. One couple had barely finished their intricate dance when the commentator barked out, "Lacks artistry!" Although bolstering our status by dismissing the efforts of others is presented as normal behavior by our culture, the feeling of superiority it produces is hollow. In contrast, mutual respect and appreciation among competitors breed a sense of solidarity.

The Insight Meditation Society once held a retreat for our board members, during which a consultant we were working with gave us an exercise. We were separated into pairs to play a game resembling tic-tac-toe. Each player was to tally his or her points. Most of us figured we were competing against our partner to see who could score more points. But one of the pairs got the idea that if they cooperated rather than competed and pooled their points, their combined score would be higher than everyone else's. Unlike the rest of us, who had assumed that every twosome would have a winner and a loser, this cooperative pair decided not to play as if they were battling each other. They outscored the rest of us because they had chosen to work together.

Competition is natural, a part of the human arsenal for survival, but when it creates enmity, we need to question its power in our lives. This is where *sympathetic joy*—joy in the happiness of others—comes in. If we're in a competitive frame of mind, when something good happens to someone else, we think it somehow diminishes us. It doesn't really, of course, but being consumed with jealousy and envy clouds our judgment. Even when we're not in the running, extreme competitiveness makes us feel as if we were.

However, if we approach other people's successes with an attitude of sympathetic joy, we can genuinely and wholeheartedly receive happiness from their good fortune. Instead of running an internal monologue that goes something like, *Oh no, you got that, but it was meant for me! It should be mine, and you took it away,* we can accept that the prize was never ours and rejoice in the other person's success. If we approach life from a place of scarcity, a mind-set that emphasizes what we lack instead of what we have, then anyone who has something we want becomes the enemy. But when we can rejoice in other people's happiness, we realize that joy and fulfillment are not finite quantities we have to grab while we can. They are always available because they are internal qualities that flow naturally if we allow them to.

An accessible path to sympathetic joy runs through

compassion, or the movement of the heart in response to pain or suffering with the wish to relieve that suffering. Compassion is an energized and empowering quality. As Buddhist monk Nyanaponika Thera says, "It is compassion that removes the heavy bar, opens the door to freedom, makes the narrow heart as wide as the world. Compassion takes away from the heart the inert weight, the paralyzing heaviness; it gives wings to those who cling to the lowlands of self."[2] Looking closely at the life of someone we consider to be the competition, we are bound to see hardships that the person has endured, or understand how tenuous status and good fortune can be. When we can connect with a perceived enemy on the level of human suffering, winning or losing seems less important.

A few years ago I led a meditation group at an elementary school in Washington, D.C. The walls of the school corridors were plastered with homilies: *Treat people the way you would like to be treated. Play fair. Don't hurt others on the inside or the outside.* The message that stopped me short, however, was *Everyone Can Play.*

Everyone Can Play is now the precept I live by. We may not agree with one another. We may argue. We may compete. But everybody gets to play, no matter what. We all deserve a shot at life.

Co-creating the Enemy

Our perception of others as enemies is influenced by how we have interacted with them in the past and how they have interacted with us. Our view of them is seldom an objective reflection of their qualities but tends to be a projection of

---

2   Nyanaponika Thera. "The Four Sublime States: Contemplations on Love, Compassion, Sympathetic Joy and Equanimity," Access to Insight, 4 April 2011, http://www.accesstoinsight.org/lib/authors/nyanaponika/wheel006.html.

our own aversion. Maybe someone harmed us in the past, so now we are afraid of them. Maybe we did something a person didn't like, so now they are angry with us. We have a mental template of what we consider harmful, injurious, and frightening, and, with or without provocation, we project that onto people, turning them into enemies. When someone looks unpleasant or threatening—when they fit our mental image of a frightening person—then we assume they intend to harm us, and we can't wait to get rid of them. And if we can't get rid of them, we feel frustrated and angry, which reinforces our view of them as an enemy.

The last thing most of us want to hear is that we might have any responsibility for creating our own enemies. After all, it wasn't *our* car that drove over our newly sodded lawn. And *we're* not the ones who spread that malicious gossip about a loved one, nor are we the one who seemed to take great pleasure in stealing a colleague's clients. But if we are ever to get rid of our enemies, or at least render them powerless over us, we will have to own up to our part in creating the enmity.

Every person has the potential to be unpleasant and harmful, just as every person has the potential to be pleasant and helpful. Think of someone you love dearly; if you look back, you can probably find a time when they did something that harmed you, even unwittingly, or a time when you were angry with them or they were angry with you.

"Enemy," then, is not a fixed definition, a label permanently affixed to anyone we believe has harmed us. It's a temporary identity we assign people when they don't do what we want or they do something we don't want. But whatever others have or have not done, enemy-making always comes back to us.

ENEMY-MAKING

A friend who was raised as a Christian once told me that from a very young age, whenever he heard the commandment "Love thy neighbor as thyself," his heart would soar. Then inevitably, his next thought would be the troubled question: *But how?*

How, indeed. What if you actually hate your neighbor, or are afraid of them, or simply find them unappealing? What if you actually hate yourself, or don't find much good about your actions when you evaluate your day? What if all too often, when confronted by a decidedly unneighborly world, you feel defensive, hostile, cut off, and alone? We can start unraveling this response by looking at our conditioning.

We have a strong urge to dichotomize human beings, to separate them into opposing categories. Stereotyping is an evolutionary mechanism designed to enhance survival, a form of shorthand for getting by in a dangerous world. We try to manage the messiness of life by creating an orderly zone of recognizable types characterized by certain traits that are associated, however loosely. Then we generalize our preconceived typologies to all members of a class or group or nation.

The problem is that once we have organized everyone into tidy categories, we may be unwilling to look beyond those labels. We commonly designate our own group as the norm, the Ins, while everyone else is the Other. Designating our own family or group as the standard, while assigning everyone else to categories that are somehow inferior, boosts our feeling of self-worth. But it also locks us into the Us-versus-Them mind-set, virtually assuring us an unending supply of enemies.

Familiarity can stop this cycle of enemy-making. A recent study of prejudice revealed that mutual trust can catch on and spread between different racial groups just as quickly as suspicion does.[3] Through something known as the "extended-contact effect," amity travels like a benign virus through opposing groups. This effect is so powerful that, according to researchers at the University of Massachusetts, bias can evaporate in a matter of hours. Peaceful exposure to the Other, the "enemy," is key. As just one example, a Palestinian-Jewish summer camp known as Oseh Shalom–Sanea al-Salam enables Jewish and Arab youths and their families to spend time together in shared activities and dialogue amid natural surroundings. Such organizations offer clues to how larger-scale initiatives might be devised to break down the Us-versus-Them stockade.

We have to be able to enlarge the perspective with which we view the world if we hope to become truly empathic. Think of the Dalai Lama learning about Christianity from Desmond Tutu and Archbishop Tutu learning about Buddhism from the Dalai Lama. Neither of these spiritual masters appears to be out to convert the other, nor do they need to agree in order to feel connected. Each maintains strong loyalty to his own traditions, creed, and people, but they are very good friends who are not constrained by the cult of either/or.

Taking action toward the good is the best way to expand our attention and dissolve the boundary of Us-versus-Them. Even simple things like working in a soup kitchen and helping feed the hungry, or having thoughtful conversations with the people next door, can ease feelings of separation from those who are unlike us on the surface.

---

3   "Tolerance over Race Can Spread, Studies Find," *The New York Times,* November 6, 2008, http://www.nytimes.com.

By aligning ourselves with issues larger than our own selfish concerns—"turning off the Me and turning on the We," as Jonathan Haidt puts it—we transcend alienation through simple human contact. In the spirit of "Love thy neighbor as thyself," more and more people start to seem like our neighbors, and we learn in real terms how to love them.

Once we divide the world into Us and Them, self and other, "other" is filled with potential enemies. Even others we love right now may turn into enemies later on. All they have to do is harm or displease us in some way, and immediately we will fear and dislike them.

How we deal with our outer enemies, then, is to see them as human beings and to see ourselves from their perspective, being conscious of our own prejudices and preoccupations, and realizing that our enemies are operating out of their own prejudices and preoccupations. "Working with the Outer Enemy," an exercise in the Appendix on page 158, will show you how you create outer enemies and how to reverse that process.

When it comes down to it, the outer enemy is a distraction. Focusing on someone who seems to have it in for us allows us to ignore the real enemy, the enemy within. But when we can see the enemy's hatred as a challenge, it becomes a spur to our own growth, a gift to wake us from our complacency.

THE POWER OF
FORGIVENESS

How do we forgive those who have hurt us? How is it possible to reconcile our differences with individuals who have done us harm or hurt our families or those responsible for committing deliberate acts of violence? Is forgiveness imperative in all cases? Or is forgiveness a spiritual absolute we wrestle with but nearly always fall short of, unable to leave grievances behind or let bygones be bygones?

There are no simple answers to these questions. We should not be sentimental about forgiveness: it is often a difficult, knotty spiritual practice that requires us to move beyond an intensely felt but self-destructive mind-set, like swallowing a bitter pill. Furthermore, we commonly use the word *forgiveness* in an imperative sense, rendering it both compulsory and difficult. We are told, for example, that until we forgive, we will never heal. We forget that forgiveness is a grieving process that often includes the expression and release of negative emotions, especially disappointment and anger. It's no use trying to avoid these painful feelings. Forgiveness that is insincere, forced, or premature can be more psychologically damaging than authentic bitterness and rage.

Helen Whitney, the director of the documentary film *Forgiveness: A Time to Love and a Time to Hate*, has said, "We talk about forgiveness as if it were one thing. Instead, we should talk about *forgivenesses*. There are as many ways to forgive as there are people needing to be forgiven. We have a cultural tendency to want to turn forgiveness into a single, universally desirable thing. But forgiveness is more complex than that."

This is important to understand. Like any form of healing, forgiveness has its own timetable and should not be rushed or engineered. We cannot force ourselves to "forgive!" any more than we can force ourselves to "let go!" What we can do is create the conditions in which forgiveness is likely to happen, beginning with full acknowledgment of the situation and how we are feeling. Until we are honest with ourselves about our pain or resentment, we cannot hope to leave it behind. Weaned on the notion that forgiveness is a selfless act executed for others at our own expense, we forget that compassion begins at home and that we must attend to our own wounds before we can open our hearts to others.

Many people confuse forgiveness with selflessness and wonder why they can't seem to manage it. In attempting to transcend their own experience and "do the right thing," many well-meaning people discover that they cannot forgive if they leave themselves out of the equation. When we understand forgiveness as a compassionate act toward ourselves that we extend to others as we're able, we begin to grasp what Helen Whitney means by forgivenesses in the plural. Every situation requires its own skillful resolution. If we wait until our motives are completely pure and residual feelings are a thing of the past, chances are we will forgive little in our lives. On the other hand, when we can see forgiveness as a survival tool, as well as a spiritual act, our requirements and self-expectations shrink to more realistic proportions.

Whether or not we hold that some acts are unforgivable, there is no doubt that some are so consequential that they can't easily be included in any conventional approach to forgiveness. This does not mean that we can't get beyond the actions of our enemies. As one Holocaust survivor put it, "I will never forget, and I will never forgive. But I brought up my children to love and not to hate."

After having survived that kind of trauma, the commitment to teach your children to love instead of hate is testimony to inherent human goodness. Such "compartmentalized forgiveness," in which we honor our authentic and pained feelings at the same time that we practice moving beyond the harm, informed the reaction of one 9/11 survivor on learning of the death of Osama bin Laden. Quoted on Andrew Sullivan's blog, *The Dish*, the writer said:

> . . . I was on the 62nd floor of Tower One when the first plane struck, and I was in the police command center in [World Trade Center Building 5] when WTC 2 collapsed on top of us. I am also a Catholic.
>
> When I turned away from the Mets-Phillies game [on TV] Sunday night to watch the President "announce" the news that everyone already seemed to know, I had no mixed emotions. That son a bitch killed my friends, colleagues, fellow New Yorkers, fellow Americans, fellow human beings. Worse still, he inspired thousands, if not more, to take up a blind nihilism as their credo, ostensibly in the name of Allah, "the merciful, the compassionate." All the pain he has brought to this world has not been reckoned and may not be reckoned in our lifetimes. I sat on my couch Sunday night and poured a large glass of Irish whiskey and toasted the death of the man who had tried to kill me. . . .
>
> Then I went upstairs and looked in on my three sleeping children—my oldest born in 2002—and I kissed them all. Then I settled in next to my wife—my beautiful wife, who will be married to me ten years tomorrow and who is carrying our fourth child. She for many long hours thought her husband of five months was crushed to death in the towers. I put my hand upon her belly and I closed my eyes and I prayed that Osama bin Laden would know the fullness of Christ's mercy.[4]

---

4   "Forgiving Bin Laden, CTD," The Dish, May 5, 2011, http://dish.andrewsullivan.com/.

I know so many people whose lives have been touched by violence: a friend whose nephew was murdered; a friend whose niece was murdered; another friend whose daughter was murdered; a score of people who have escaped abusive relationships, or have been raped, or have a history of terrible sexual or physical abuse in their childhoods. I have learned from them all that in dealing with our enemies, we need not become agents of revenge with closed hearts and constricted minds; we need not dedicate the rest of our lives to the downfall of those who have wronged us. They have shown me that we can devote ourselves to fostering change—for children, for women, for elders, for anyone vulnerable or afraid—rather than fixating on revenge.

For some that has meant that instead of obsessing on how to make wrongdoers suffer, they focus on standing up for the disenfranchised, for people who feel so hopeless, so deprived of dignity and social support that they lash out at others in the belief that nobody cares about them. Otherwise, these activists say, we remain part of the problem, perpetuating violence in the name of justice, reacting without mindfulness to personal grudges and the seductive call for retribution.

They have taught me that our lives don't need to be dedicated to getting even. If we can let go of that burning need and our fixation on anger, then we can start to understand the possibility of actually experiencing the generative power of compassion. The force of compassion drives us toward life, openness, renewal, and love. This is how our enemies become our greatest spiritual teachers.

CHAPTER 2

Victory over the Inner Enemy

There are too many times in life when we just cannot avoid losing our temper. Someone attacks or provokes us, we feel that excitement is the only way to avoid being crippled by fear in a tough situation, we just can't stand something that is happening to us or to others, and we blow our top. Sometimes our heated action seems to help; we get the immediate result we want. But even then, usually we feel bad afterward, we realize that our overreaction will cause more problems down the line, we become exhausted, we lose a potential friend, and we have populated our universe with an even more dangerous potential enemy. As we mature and gain more experience with the negative results and side effects of the anger habit, we shift our priorities, and we resolve to improve our mastery of our emotional reactions. We tire of being whipped about by uncontrollable inner impulses, and we decide we really have to be the master of our forceful energies, and not be mastered by them. We then are ready to face our inner enemies.

There are all too many of them, a host of powerful forces within our minds, obsessive desire, burning anger, haunting jealousy, stressful competitiveness, foolish pride, stubborn delusion, and self-righteous conviction. They are addictive energies, in that they take hold of us from within by seeming to enhance our energy and expand our being, only to let us down all too soon and leave us in an even more vulnerable situation. The Buddhist word for them (Sanskrit *klesha,* Pali *kilesa*) comes from the verb root *klish-,* which means "twist" or "torment." They harm us without fail and so definitely qualify as enemies.

Of all of them, anger is the ultimate inner enemy. It is unimaginably destructive. One of my Buddhist teachers, Tara Tulku, used to say that the most important component of a nuclear bomb is anger fueled by hatred. What impels a human being to press the button, turn the key, pull the trigger on unimaginable physical destruction is the mind of hatred rising into anger. It is important to recognize that in a full evaluation of consequential action, *thought is action.* It not only motivates physical action, it *is* physical action, however subtle. It has consequences in the physical world, and it shapes the positive or negative evolutionary changes in the lives of the thinker who acts in the mind. Indeed, based on the insight that thought is the most powerful act of all, spiritual and psychological traditions worldwide rely on mental sciences to decrease the influence of negative thoughts and to shape thoughts in positive ways.

Anger is the wish to obliterate the target. It is the hot flash of destructive momentum that makes people lash out and, in too many cases, recklessly destroy lives, destroy the environment, destroy the very way of life of those perceived to be the enemy. In the Buddhist teachings, it is said that one moment of hatred against an enlightened being produces eons of negative effects, leading the hating person into a season in hell.

Anger is like a powerful addiction. We're addicted to anger as a state of being and a way of acting in the world. But if we are to have any peace, we must recognize hatred and anger as potentially lethal compulsions that we have to kick. Like any addict, we have to realize the full power of these mental impulses in order to truly resolve to free ourselves from them.

We must not be confused by the thought that sometimes anger has a positive use, such as impelling us to take action against injustice. In fact, critical judgment and ethical commitment are what inspire us to act to correct injustice, and if anger goes along with them, it tends to make that action ineffective. But such kinds of rationalization are how addictive substances keep their hold on us. It would be like saying that because heroin is sometimes used for end-of-life palliative care, addiction to heroin is not all that bad. We must decide that anger and hatred serve no useful purpose and that for all intents and purposes they are categorically destructive, even though sometimes their harmful effects do not appear immediately. Even if we do decide that anger is bad for us, like any addiction, to reach the point of resolving definitely to eliminate it, we need to know precisely what we're dealing with. Anger arises when mounting irritation, annoyance, and frustration burst into an irresistible impulse to respond in a harmful manner to the perceived source of those feelings. In the grip of anger, we are no longer the master of our thoughts, speech, or actions. Once this happens, we are not "expressing our anger," as is often said to justify a supposedly healthy release; rather, we have become the involuntary instrument of our rage. No longer in control of it, we have become its effect. Who would choose to be angry in that manner if they could stay in control of their feelings and act skillfully even when the target is annoying? Wouldn't we prefer that our judgment remain clear, while we still maintain free choice in our actions? Our anger or hatred only results in violent outbursts when we're inflamed with rage and our good sense has gone out the window. This kind of anger, being "mad," that is, insane in its fury, destroys all in its path, not least our own emotional balance.

If the first step toward release from our addiction to anger is deciding that we must break the cycle, there is nobody better to help us go cold turkey than the great 8th-century Indian sage Shantideva, a Buddhist mind scientist at the renowned

Nalanda University. He is best known as the author of the *Bodhicharyavatara (Introduction to the Bodhisattva Conduct)*, a practical text originally written in Sanskrit verse that has become so popular in the West that it has already appeared in several translations into English and other European languages. His teaching of tolerance and compassion is considered to contain the supreme Buddhist methodology of developing love and compassion for all beings.

In the Tibetan tradition, the teaching is thought to have come down through a lineage of living masters that has continued unbroken from the Buddha's time until today, with Shantideva having been perhaps the most eloquent author in that lineage. The present Fourteenth Dalai Lama of Tibet is generally considered to be the main living holder of that teaching lineage, and anyone who has ever been moved by His Holiness's discourses on compassion has met that living tradition.[5] Shantideva helps motivate us by convincing us that being angry is like biting the hand that feeds us: for example, he likens the madness of fury to venting our anger on a bodhisattva, a being who has only our best interest at heart. This is patently self-destructive—why would we revile someone who wants only to benefit us? It is like being angry with Jesus or Mary or Moses or Muhammad, or even God—in other words, being angry with a being that one considers to be the source of all goodness.

Anger and hatred connect to what many consider to be the supreme of all evils. In all cultural imaginations, the devil—the very embodiment of evil—thrives on inflicting pain and torture by means of malevolent actions. And since his motivation to harm others consists of the mental impulses of anger and hatred, it is clear that such evil is rooted in anger and hatred; they are the source of all evil acts. In the Buddhist biological

---

5   There are a number of reasonable translations of Shantideva's Guide available in English. The Dalai Lama's *Flash of Lightning in the Dark of Night* is a good commentary, and my books *Anger* and also *Infinite Life* can be considered commentaries on some of the key sections of his book.

theory of karma, addiction to anger and hatred leads eventually to rebirth in one of the 32 hells, which are described in the
literature in the most terrifyingly lurid detail.

Anger and hatred want their victim to feel pain and suffering, while love and compassion want their beloved to feel joy
and happiness. The ultimate opposite of anger is love, the fer-
vent wish for others to be happy. But at the inner-enemy stage,
when we're still learning to manage our addiction to anger,
aiming for love pushes us too far. It is unrealistic to expect to
immediately switch from anger and hate to compassion and
love. Patience is the middle ground, the place of tolerance, forbearance, and in time, forgiveness. We might still be irritated
when we are harmed (or think we are harmed), but we will not
lose ourselves to anger so long as we can tolerate the irritation,
be patient with the harm and the harmer, refrain from reacting vengefully, and maybe even forgive the injury. Patience is
the antidote to anger, and love can freely arise on the basis of
patience as the ultimate opposite of hate. So, to deal with the
inner enemy, our positive resolve is to cultivate patience.

ANGER

Anger is the opposite of lovingkindness, the spirit of
boundless friendship toward ourselves and others. Anger
and aversion cause us to strike out against what is happening in an effort to remain separate from it. Anger
causes us to define what is going on in the moment as
unbearable: "I can't stand to be with things as they are."

Anger takes many forms, from guilt, fear, and hostility to impatience, disappointment, and anxiety. We
tend to misunderstand anger and our responses to it. It
is sometimes hard to balance the need to acknowledge
anger rather than be afraid of it against the knowledge
that acting on anger—or worse, being ruled by it—can

have damaging, even dire, consequences. In order to be whole human beings, we need to cultivate awareness of exactly what we are feeling and how we are responding. When emotions are unacceptable to us, we often engage in self-deception in order to distance ourselves from them. Only when we can fully acknowledge powerful emotions like anger will we develop self-understanding.

The Buddha said, "Anger with its poisoned source and fevered climax is murderously sweet." Indeed. But with the murderous sweetness comes pain. The satisfaction of an angry outburst is extremely short lived. No less painful, however, is the feeling of disconnection and isolation we get from denying our anger, which distances us from the world around us. Overwhelmed by anger, we try to alleviate our pain by separating ourselves from the offending person or situation. This is a recipe for loneliness, walling us off within the confines of reactivity and rage.

Anger, like a forest fire, burns up its own support, the Buddha said. It leaves us bereft, destroying our well-being and stranding us far from where we want to be. Think about what happens when we are overcome by anger. First, we isolate the enemy—the problem or person or situation—and fixate on it unrelentingly. Lost in this angry state, we develop tunnel vision, unable to see a way out. Completely forgetting the law of change—"This too shall pass," as the old proverb has it—we lock the problem and ourselves into a box of perceived permanence ("This is how it is and this is how it's always going to be"). Unable to see alternatives or imagine a truth larger than our immediate grievance or pain, we end up feeling helpless and overwhelmed.

Still, I would argue that anger can have its uses. When we are confronted with cruelty or injustice, anger can help us burn off the fog of apathy. When we are confronted with our own inner demons, anger in the form of exasperation may prompt us to make changes that self-coddling failed to motivate. When we find ourselves in a situation where we feel unseen, unheard, or unappreciated, frustration may jolt us awake and give us the courage to speak up. Anger can dispel blind spots and help us see beyond social niceties: sometimes the angry person in the room is the one speaking truth to power or refusing to accept hypocrisy. In sum, anger can be a positive force when we learn to harness its truth-seeking power without becoming lost in self-righteousness or explosive fury. But despite all of anger's potential good points, the skillful use of it is the exception rather than the rule. Far more often—indeed, nearly always—anger narrows the mind and shuts down the heart, leaving us confused, bitter, and alone.

Mindfulness practice opens up a world of options for working with anger. Normally, we get lost in the story and identify with the anger: *They did this, so I'm going to do that, and my vengeful act will destroy them.* Or we may go the way of self-condemnation: *I'm such a terrible person; I'm so awful; I can't believe I'm still angry. I've been in therapy for ten years, so how could I still be angry? Maybe it's the wrong kind of therapy.*

But using mindfulness we can say, "Oh, it's anger. This is anger." If we can maintain that sort of balance, then we are able to take the anger apart and see into its nature. And what do we see? We see anger's composite, conditioned, and ever-changing nature. We see that it contains many emotions—sadness, fear, helplessness, anxiety— woven together. None of those emotions feels good, but at least they show us we are dealing with a living system. Then, if we decide to speak or to act, we can do so from a place of acknowledging all those feelings and not just the top layer, the anger.

Gaining insight into the nature of the anger, we also perceive the nature of change. We appreciate the evanescence of feelings that seem so solid and intractable. Knowing that they will pass decreases their power to take over our mind, something we may never before have appreciated, since we were so busy reacting. Instead of catching ourselves 15 regrettable actions after we first felt angry, we develop a visceral sensitivity to what's happening within us in the moment, and through mindfulness, we can shape our reaction right away.

To deepen our determination to eliminate anger and hatred from our stock of impulsive drives, we need only reflect on how we feel when we are gripped by anger in its first explosive moments and how sickened we are by hatred festering within us even after our fury has cooled down. Once we have given in to anger, once we feel justified in hating, our energy is constantly disturbed. Even when something distracts us into feeling a moment of pleasure, soon a thought of hatred about the unbearable person or situation intrudes and spoils our good mood. The grandchild or best friend or loved one who normally delights us by their very presence suddenly seems irritating, their affection too cloying, their presence a waste of time, as our mind yearns to get back to calculating how we can destroy whoever or whatever has made us angry—the victim of our hating thoughts. At night, sleep will not come easily because we are so jacked up with frustration that we can't get back at our enemy.

Physiologically, the state of anger and hatred produces a stress hormone, cortisol, which breaks down body tissues and upsets our blood chemistry and circulatory system. People living in a constant state of irritation or rage are at risk for high blood pressure, strokes, and heart attacks, and they are prone to arthritis from inflammation of the joints. The more we look at the science of anger and understand rage as the granddaddy of destructive emotions, the more powerful our determination becomes to free ourselves from its obsessive clutches. Shantideva calls a mind held by anger and hatred a "wounded" mind. Anger and hatred wound us in body, mind, and spirit.

When something or someone has injured us, Shantideva says, the anger we feel is a second injury, wounding us from within. Your mind cannot rest as anger toward the one who harmed you stirs within you the desire for revenge. Things that ordinarily bring you pleasure, even joy—the face of your beloved, good food, enchanting entertainment, sensual delight—all lose their appeal the minute you become angry. When you are really angry, your mind replays the injury again and again, plotting how to retaliate in kind or worse.

Anger is like fire—explosive, burning. Other times, hate can be frozen, like dry ice, only to explode again when your victim comes near. Anger spoils relationships where there should be great reciprocity. Even those who depend on us for their livelihood and dignity will grow to hate us and will wait for a chance to hurt or even destroy us if we constantly subject them to our anger.

You may have a loving family, close friends, partners in business, or mates in an adventure, but if you periodically blow up at them, real affection will be tempered or even destroyed. I know this all too well, having had a very bad temper from youth. Bullied by my older brother, I used a show of furious temper to attempt to defend myself. In that way I became addicted to anger. But I didn't have the force or the destructive intent to really frighten or hurt my brother, whom in fact I idolized, so the more furious I became, the less impressive my display of temper would be. Addictive substances are like that: when you overuse them and become dependent upon them, they cease to give you a kick. This is the ultimate deception. Anger and hatred appear to help you, to give you strength, but in the end they make your circumstances more difficult, weakening you in the process. Meanwhile, holding anger and hatred in your being, allowing them to shape your outlook, destroys you slowly from within.

Recently I met an old friend, a woman with whom I share many views, particularly our opinion of some misguided world leaders. But my friend, I noticed, has been nursing anger and hatred toward them for too long, and when she went into ranting mode, even though she was preaching to the converted, all her outburst did was contort her face, revealing the disjointedness of her emotions. It made me very sad to see a beautiful face burned up with frenzied anger and impotent rage. She felt bad, and everyone who listened to her felt bad. She was clearly unable to advance her agenda of reform effectively because she was so given over to anger and hatred. No longer able to help her cause in any useful way, she herself had become part of the problem. This sort of rage may well be why violent revolutions often result in even more oppressive leadership than the regime they replaced.

Any enemy who attacks us does so only as a tool of hatred and anger. And when we counterattack angrily, the devil of hatred has found another victim in ourselves. We also become the tool of anger, just as our enemy was, and the devil of hatred has a field day watching us destroy each other. Whenever anger and hatred are involved, they always emerge the winner. The only way out of this vicious circle is to recognize that the real enemy is anger itself. This is the enemy I must defeat to find my real friend, happiness.

Once you understand that anger itself is your greatest enemy, it simplifies the struggle to discover happiness. Since your main enemy is within, you can turn on it, find its root, learn its manifestations, armor yourself against it, and work to uproot it. Then you will be free of its harm. You can conquer it bit by bit to achieve the happiness you seek.

This is the radical discovery of Buddhist psychology. We don't have to resign ourselves to continual suffering, helpless not only before our outer enemies but also, more important, before our own inner drives, our impulses and demands. You need not give up and simply allow yourself to be buffeted here and there by your passions. You can become conscious of what you were formerly unconscious of. You can understand your drives, see where they come from, and then block that source and reclaim that energy for your own positive use, for your own happiness and the happiness of your loved ones.

PATIENCE

Patience doesn't, as we commonly assume, mean dull endurance but rather holding a much bigger picture of life. Patience involves recognizing how we can carry on—even flourish—through ups and downs, twists and turns, triumphs and tragedies.

Cultivating patience doesn't imply becoming apathetic or succumbing to feelings of powerlessness. Instead, we remember the simple truth of our lack of sovereignty over unfolding events. Patience is peaceful awareness in the midst of weathering life's storms, giving us the ability to go on in the face of adversity.

In Buddhist teaching this quality is likened to equanimity. Equanimity isn't about not caring about what does or doesn't happen to us or to others. Of course, we care. Rather, equanimity, as the voice of wisdom, simply reminds us that life is a series of highs and lows over which we have little control. We can and should do everything we can to ease suffering and foster happiness in others. But in the end, the universe is not ours to manage. And even as change unfolds, the pace of it might not match our timetable. Acknowledging this brings insight to our compassion, and realism and sustainability to our efforts to make a difference in the world.

I am inspired by Larry Brilliant, who as a young doctor

in India in the 1970s was a significant figure in the successful campaign to eradicate smallpox. Larry visited temples where Hindus prayed to the goddess of smallpox for assistance, looking for unreported outbreaks; trekked to jungle villages in 120-degree heat; painted public health notices on the sides of elephants and rickshaws; and vaccinated and treated thousands of patients. When the World Health Organization declared the world free of smallpox in 1980, Larry sent his friends an unforgettable postcard, with a devastating picture of the last victim on one side and a blessing from his spiritual teacher on the other. It sang out a glorious hallelujah that echoed around the world.

A few years ago, I was walking in New York City, my head filled with that morning's news of anticipated terror and the appalling prospect of smallpox returning as a weapon, born again to the world through hatred and fear. Suddenly I thought of Larry, of his postcard, and of the despair he would likely feel on seeing the most loving and effective work of his lifetime threatened and maybe destroyed. Later that day, when I telephoned him, I found that although he was filled with dismay at even the thought of terrorists reviving an extinct disease, his amazing spirit was undaunted. "We eradicated it once," he said. "We can do it again."

Once we are truly determined to win our freedom from anger and hatred, we need to understand their mental mechanics. Here is where there is a big difference between Shantideva's teaching and the teachings of many religious authorities (including some Buddhists) that simply call for the suppression of anger as a "deadly sin." Rather than telling us merely to suppress anger, Shantideva's psychological manual helps us delve into the whole question of anger and gain awareness of how it works when it is teamed up with hatred. This is a more active approach.

Included in the definition of anger as an addiction is its ability to carry us away. We are carried away when addictive passion demolishes our reason and common sense, and makes our mind, speech, and body its tools. Using mindful awareness, we observe how anger arises. When we do, we quickly see that anger doesn't just explode without warning. There is a phase during which you begin to feel very uncomfortable, with tightness in your solar plexus and a choking sensation in your throat, and sometimes even with a nauseous feeling in your stomach and a flush of heat. You experience strong physical and mental discomfort. Before real anger happens, there is a kind of mental discomfort or frustration that comes with the awareness that something is happening that you don't want or that what you do want is being thwarted. Though you become more and more irritated with the situations, you are still reasonable at this point.

The key is to intervene mentally, verbally, or physically as soon as possible, to dissipate your internal discomfort or engage the external situation energetically. This is the time to act forcefully and powerfully, not to suppress your feelings of discomfort. In this moment, before your frustration bursts into anger, you tend to be vividly aware, your judgment about the causal processes involved in anger is sound, and you have a chance to act effectively.

If there is something physical or verbal you can do about the external situation, you can do it with urgency and forcefulness. Because of your intensity, some people may see your actions as fueled by anger. But in fact, you are not yet angry, you have not lost control. By being mindful and finding that momentary gap before reactivity takes over, you exhibit a force that is controlled, measured, and well-aimed, responding with the elegance and grace of a martial artist. If you cannot act physically or verbally because the other people involved in the situation cannot be effectively influenced, you can redirect your mind to defuse your discomfort and frustration, using that energy to develop mental immunity to the situation. You can use your pain from whatever harm you have received to evolve creatively within yourself, without either losing your temper or suppressing your rage to fester within as icy hatred. You resolve to direct your mind to develop greater tolerance, to empathize with the agents of harm to broaden your understanding of their situation to see what made them harmful, i.e. given over to their own anger and hate, and to deepen your determination never to act that way yourself and cause such pain to any other.

If you act outwardly, your active engagement will be much more effective if you are reasonable and in control of your energy than if you are out of control and overreacting. It is always possible that whatever you do, you will be unable to affect the outcome, and what you fear the most will happen after all. But in that case, you can turn and intervene in your inner world, in your mind.

Regardless of the outcome, it is imperative to remain cheerful. That doesn't mean putting on a false face, suppressing your discomfort and frustration, and pretending to be oh, so cheerful, when really you're feeling more and more agitated. That approach never works. But when you move assertively to change the situation while there is still hope that your intervention can be effective, you will be appropriately forceful, even aggressive if necessary, to make a point. But when you can't do anything external, when circumstances are too dire and your power of intervention is too weak, you must work internally to change your perception of the situation so you don't react.

"But how can I change my perception of a situation that isn't going as I want?" you might ask. There are a number of ways. For one, you can distract yourself by counting your blessings—thinking about how things could be even worse. Or you can look more deeply at what is bothering you and question your interpretation of it. Interpretation is always operating subliminally, affecting your perception of what seems to be objective fact. To make your perception more realistic, you can use critical investigation to erode your certainty about what is actually happening. Then you can begin to change your feelings about it. You then have the room to see how the seeming disadvantage of having your hopes and desires thwarted can instead be used to your advantage. You can take the occasion to develop your tolerance and strength. Once you see through your sense of certainty about what's wrong, you can view the situation from another perspective and take a disadvantage as a challenge to be mastered. At a minimum, you will realize that getting upset is not going to improve the situation; it will only add to your frustration and unhappiness.

Changing your perception, however you accomplish it, is crucial, since you are dealing with an addiction. Just as substance addicts are seduced into thinking that the substance will relieve their bad feeling, anger presents itself to your mind as your own helpful energy. It speaks within you as the thought, *This situation is unacceptable, outrageous! I should explode with fury, and my fiery energy will burn away the obstacle, clear up the situation.* Maybe that solution worked in the past, but now it's essential to see what else you can do about the pain you are experiencing.

OUR NATURALLY RADIANT MIND

There's a very beautiful teaching in which the Buddha said, "The mind is by nature radiant. It's shining. It is because of visiting forces that we suffer." One of the things I have always found breathtaking in Buddhist teaching is its inclusivity. The Buddha didn't say that some people's minds are radiant and pure but yours, well, not so much. He said that everybody's mind is radiant and pure. And the Buddha did not say that, because of these visiting forces, we are bad people. He said that, because of them, we suffer.

We know these forces well—anger, greed, grasping, jealousy, and fear among them. Sometimes when they arise, we give them all our power. They take over, define the moment, and define our sense of who we are and all that we will ever be. Or we feel frightened or aggrieved at their arrival, dismayed that once again we can not control what comes to visit. (Though, really, how could we have controlled it?)

Whether we let our negative visitors take us over or we push them away, we suffer. Caught in their embrace, we identify with these unwholesome mind-states, either projecting those bad feelings onto others and creating enemies in the world, or making an enemy of ourselves with thoughts like, *I am such a jealous person, and I always will be. This is who I really am.* Once we give in to the visitors, we lose any choice in the matter: we're locked into a negative state of mind.

Next time you are visited by a negative force—fear or anger, for example—experiment with a different perspective. Instead of thinking of the visiting force as the enemy and rejecting it, or rejecting yourself for entertaining it, see it simply as *suffering.* That will give you a very different relationship to the fear or anger, one that is rooted in compassion. We can cultivate a mind free of enmity toward our thoughts and feelings, while at the same time avoid being overcome by them.

Addiction to a mental habit is subtler than addiction to a physical substance like drugs or alcohol or food, or a behavior like gambling or compulsive sex. A mental habit comes to you as an imperative of your own nature; hence it is all the more irresistible. As an anger addict you have experienced the rush, the high of expressing anger, as well as the dreadful crash after you have acted on your anger, which only made things worse. Still, in the moment of temptation, you may set aside this memory as you get caught up in the promise of the rush. This is where the recognition of anger as an enemy becomes all-important and the yoga of taming anger begins. It is essential to return to your decision that anger must be eliminated.

Here Shantideva's classic maxim is appropriate, adding as well a touch of humor (always a good weapon in the battle against anger): "Why be unhappy about something if you can do something about it? If you can't do anything about it, why be unhappy about it?"

Why be unhappy about anything ever, in other words? When you are frustrated, you can intervene in the situation before you get angry, and do it cheerfully, with a joyous energy. When there is nothing external to be done, then you can intervene within yourself, reminding yourself not to increase your unhappiness by adding bitterness to your frustration.

Herein lies the difference between an enlightened, psychologically astute approach to anger and a conventional approach in which suppressing manifestations of anger is the main objective. Women in particular are raised and socialized to suppress anger and aggressiveness. Meanwhile, they often suffer general oppression, having to live in a state of constant frustration. As progressive as Western culture is supposed to be, women are still dominated by men, and the more awakened ones feel their anger at this is justified. So the key point is not whether women should suppress or release their anger but how skillful they can be in asserting themselves when necessary to defend themselves and their views. Too often, when women see something bad occurring, or are frustrated in trying to make something good happen, they restrain their reactions out of politeness or fear of offending; but then, when their feelings of rage become unbearable, they may explode. By that time, their actions will most likely provoke unwanted counterreactions.

Both men and women could benefit from the wisdom that they are most effective when they act forcefully while they are still feeling cool-headed.

My wife is a master of this skill. I can come home from the office upset about something that happened and eager to fill her ears with it. She will look up from what she's doing and say something like, "Why don't you just shut up before we're both upset about it?" I'm brought up short by her response, close to angry at not being listened to, but I have learned instead to relax, laugh, and keep my peace. Whatever I'm upset about is never that important anyway, and if my wife had let me run on about it until she was feeling just as annoyed as me, she might have found fault with how I handled the situation and told me so in an agitated way. And then we might have argued about what happened, unnecessarily reliving the whole situation. Instead, she helped me drop whatever I was upset about and recover my cheerfulness. This is how we can follow the profound instruction to always be happy and never lose good cheer.

Shantideva describes three kinds of patience we can cultivate to counter the inner enemy of anger: tolerant patience, insightful patience, and forgiving patience.

Tolerant Patience

Sometimes we grit our teeth and heroically tolerate suffering and pain, with a view to developing strength or health or intelligence. *No pain, no gain* is the maxim here. I might struggle to run a mile to strengthen my legs, hold a painful yoga posture to stretch my muscles, or force myself to repeat a word in a foreign language again and again in order to master the tongue. In all these cases, I can bear discomfort, even pain, with joy. This is not masochism, because my intention is not to induce pain, but I bear it willingly in order to achieve the goal I hold in mind. This is *tolerant patience.* It arms us against anger by making the threshold of explosion more and more remote.

We need to defend against hair-trigger reactions to pain and frustration. Sometimes situations make us happy spontaneously and effortlessly, but, more often, life is irritating. Things tend to go wrong: they break; we bump into them; they let us down. Other people always have their own agendas, and they often don't know what to do to make us happy, or they try to make us happy, only to end up achieving the opposite result. If we can adopt the attitude that even pain can be used to produce happiness, it goes without saying that pleasure will produce even more. We don't have to generate unnecessary pain to achieve this benefit. Day-to-day life produces quite enough to work with.

Unfortunately, it is much easier to suffer than to be happy. The causes of suffering are more numerous than the causes of happiness. Unless we come up with a positive antidote, we are bound to suffer more. Logically, then, the way to find more happiness is to take the causes that usually bring suffering and transform them into causes of happiness. With this in mind, we can take our experiences of suffering and, instead of bitterly wallowing in them, use them to develop our transcendent mind. This is the mind that aims toward perfect freedom and is willing to give up superficial pleasures and momentary happiness to achieve truly reliable happiness for the long term.

But reaching that point is easier said than done. How on earth can you turn a cause of suffering into a cause for happiness? It's a matter of shifting your aim. You have to imagine real happiness, taking any moment of release from suffering that you've ever known and multiplying it by a thousand.

But whoever said there is such a release in the first place? The Buddha did, Jesus did, and so have many other great spiritual teachers and philosophers over the centuries.

But how do we achieve it? By changing our reactions to

everything. In other words, we don't get overly excited about ordinary pleasures, and we react to pain by using it to develop tolerance. Tolerance is the small beginning of freedom from being irritated by a pain. We build that tolerance into real patience, which gets stronger and stronger under the pressure of everyday life. Tolerating discomfort gives us the ability to endure, which leads to an inner release from the force of circumstances, making real happiness possible. We develop patience not to experience fleeting pleasure but to develop transcendent detachment. Transcendent tolerance means freedom from fear of any kind of suffering. Nothing that comes our way throws us. This is the only happiness that endures.

Human beings have a tremendous capacity to adapt, to get used to things. We can build up a tolerance for almost anything, even something that at first seems intolerable, if we do it gradually, taking a little bit of it, then a bit more, repeating it again and again until eventually we no longer experience it as intolerable. Scratching an itch leads to more itching or a painful raw spot, but if we can endure an itch without scratching, eventually the itch will go away.

Normally we become frustrated with the discomfort we encounter in daily life, even with uncontrollable discomfort. Little everyday frustrations can build into explosions of anger: hating the rain, cursing the wind, writhing with fury that we've caught this or that illness, or suffered this or that assault or accident. When we face extreme suffering we shake our fist at God, fate, Buddha, Jesus, or our parents. But what's the point? Our reactions of frustration and fury do not affect nature or any divine power, or change circumstances beyond our control. They merely add internal suffering and stress to the pain and pressure we already feel. Instead, we can skillfully adapt to circumstances beyond our control, using the power of positive habit to counter the habit of angry reactions.

MAKING AN ENEMY OF SUFFERING

It is easy to turn suffering into the enemy. In the throes of emotional or physical pain, we want to be anywhere but where we are, smack up against our human condition. We tend to fight against suffering when it assails us, which only brings more pain. When suffering approaches us in other people's lives, we may do our best to avoid it. Though we have a natural impulse toward empathy and a wish to behave benevolently toward those in need, this is sometimes harder than it sounds. We don't always know how to relieve others' suffering; often we can't, in fact. Then our only recourse is to be present and attend to the suffering, which can be difficult. Confronted with the difficulty of bearing witness, we sometimes turn away from those in trouble, intimidated by our own sense of powerlessness and frightened by the challenge of allowing suffering to simply be there, without being overwhelmed by feelings of guilt or anxiety.

Until we develop a loving presence for ourselves—tenderness and trust in the face of our own inner demons—it is difficult to witness the pain of others. We may find ourselves deflecting their needs or distancing them with platitudes: "You'll feel better soon." "There's a lesson here for you to learn." "This will make you stronger." A friend told me a story about just this issue, from the early days of the AIDS crisis. During a healing circle, a man covered with Kaposi's sarcoma lesions lost his temper when a smiley-faced volunteer chirped out a New Age cliché: "Just remember that no one can make you suffer if you don't want to!" In response to these empty words, the dying man rose to his feet, exploding with rage. Until those around him could learn to sit with pain, rather than well-meaning but clueless people trying to cheer him up, he would continue to feel isolated and alone. He didn't need candy-coated lies. More than anything, this suffering man longed for simple, truthful, fearless presence in the face of his own catastrophe. He wanted to be witnessed with open eyes.

I encountered this same dynamic when a woman who had suffered a tragic loss six months earlier came to me for guidance. Her friends were becoming impatient with her, she said, implying that she should "get over it already." "My friends all have golden lives," this lady told me. "Nothing ever goes wrong for them. In their eyes, I've become this emblem of something horrible, something *outside* of them." In fact, her friends had ostracized her for their own self-protection, using suffering as the wedge between them. By turning her into the Other—one of those to whom bad things happen—they inserted a make-believe bubble of safety between themselves and the human condition.

It is highly doubtful that her friends had such perfect lives, of course. Experience has taught me that many things happen behind closed doors that people would rather not talk about. Rather than suggesting this, however, I heard myself say something I didn't expect. "I think you need new friends," I told her. "Or maybe you need to meet my friends. They are all a wreck!"

This isn't completely true: my friends aren't any more a wreck than most people. My friends and I are accustomed to being honest about our suffering. Every human being faces challenges on a regular basis: unresolved issues, free-floating fears, deep insecurity, grief. There's nothing wrong in any of this. The trouble comes when we struggle to maintain the notion that having a rough time means there is something wrong with us and that if we could make ourselves perfect enough, smart enough, wily enough, or lucky enough, we would never suffer again. This is how the ego turns ordinary pain into the enemy of suffering.

In my book *Faith*, I wrote about the suffering of my own childhood: my father's mental illness, my mother's death when I was nine, my subsequent feelings of isolation and despair. After reading the book, Bob Thurman told me, "You should never be ashamed of the suffering you've been through." His comment floored me. In that moment, I realized how much shame I had been carrying without realizing it. Bob went on to tell me how he had lost an eye in an accident in 1961 and how this experience had helped to refocus his life on finding deeper truths. Afterward, his teacher, a Mongolian monk named Geshe Wangyal, told him, "Never be ashamed of what happened to you. You have lost one eye but gained a thousand eyes of wisdom." This attitude is how we can use misfortune as a spur to awakening.

Looking around at other people, we see how some are brave and heroic under pressure or in pain, while others succumb even to less stressful circumstances. We admire the brave and scorn the timid, so this can inspire us to make a firm resolution to cultivate courage. It is much like the training a soldier undergoes. Recruits go through tremendous hardship to prepare for battle, because it gives them the best chance to survive the dangers they will face.

You are in a war with your mental addictions, especially your addiction to anger. You cannot expect to win any major conflict without taking some serious blows. Anger uses you as its tool to dish out hard knocks not only to you but to all those around you. When you turn against anger, you must expect it to turn on you. So you have to strengthen your resolve and harden yourself to it. When it turns on you, like any enemy, it wants to make you suffer. But if you have learned to tolerate suffering without taking offense at it or taking it personally, then you are fortified against whatever anger can do to you. It cannot win you over, cannot make you blow up. In this place of great endurance and great inner tolerance, you have found the way to freedom.

Heroism in battle is a metaphor for heroism in the battle against the enemy anger. Anger and fear and other mental addictions are worthy enemies, whose defeat brings the truly worthy fruit of freedom. You can only overcome these mental addictions by rising above whatever pain you suffer in battle with them. True heroism rises above the concerns of ordinary, self-centered life and even above the fear of death. Warriors fueled by anger are the minions of anger, and the anger that drives them onto the field has already taken away their freedom.

We can deploy our understanding and experience of overcoming anger to change our attitude toward suffering in general. Suffering builds character, helping us overcome pride and arrogance. It enables us to identify with others who suffer and develop true sympathy for their situation, attitudes without which we can never develop compassion, a crucial key to happiness. The paradox is that the more we are driven to focus on helping others overcome suffering, the less we focus on our own suffering and the happier we automatically become.

But in the end, we really do not like to suffer, and so we are motivated to look at the causes of suffering, discovering in the process that all too often our own negative actions and attitudes are the real enemies, the real causes of our suffering—at least they are the causes over which we have the most control. Therefore, suffering makes us want to avoid negative attitudes and actions, and to cultivate the positive insofar as possible.

If you grasp this, you are now confirmed in the first level of patience—the tolerance of suffering developed through the discipline of conscious suffering, or learning to use suffering as a spur to transcendent freedom. In your campaign to develop patience, your battle to conquer anger, you have also discovered how to use suffering to counter pride and arrogance, and enable you to identify with other suffering beings, empathize with their suffering, and want them also to be happy and free of suffering.

BIG-SKY MIND

In his teachings on compassion, the Buddha encouraged us to develop "a mind so filled with love it resembles space." Can you picture your mind being as limitless, unconstrained, free, and open as space? Spaciousness of mind and heart is a fundamental component of a resilient spirit. It brings us a kind of well-being that isn't dependent on the successes or failures we encounter on any given day. Unconditional well-being does not exclude pain but surrounds it with wisdom and love. This radical kind of happiness is the antidote to suffering. And it is available to us at any time and even in the most unlikely circumstances.

Consider what's happening at one of America's highest-security prisons, deep in the Bible Belt in Alabama.[6] The state's most violent and mentally unstable male prisoners are incarcerated in the William E. Donaldson Correctional Facility outside Birmingham. About a third of the 1,500 or so prisoners have lifetime sentences with no chance of parole, and 24 of the cells are reserved for death row. Donaldson has a history of inmate violence—both between inmates and against the prison staff. In fact, in some areas of the facility, meals are slid into inmates' cells through narrow metal boxes in the doors in order to protect the officers delivering the food.

As harsh and violent as life is in the cell blocks, inside the prison gym, it's a different story. Three times a year, for ten days, the gym is transformed into a hall for vipassana, or insight, meditation. (A follow-up three-day retreat is held once a year.) For the duration, two dozen or so inmates rise at 4 A.M. and retire at 9 P.M., meditating for much of the 17 hours in between. Led by volunteers from

---

6   The following story draws on reporting by Debbie Elliott, "At End-of-the-Line Prison, an Unlikely Escape," February 08, 2011, at http://www.npr.org, and on personal communications from Dr. David Tytell.

S. N. Goenka's Prison Trust, they eat a strict vegetarian diet, abstain from smoking, neither read nor write, and observe total silence. Apart from the occasional one-on-one with a teacher, the only "conversation" consists of the inmates' internal dialogue or examination of what's going on in their bodies and minds.

"It's a rude awakening for some prisoners," one of the teachers, Carl Franz, told a reporter for NPR's *Morning Edition*. "Everyone's mind is a kind of Pandora's Box, and when you have thirty-three rather serious convicts facing their past and their own minds, their memories, their regrets, rough childhood, their crimes, lots of stuff comes up."

That said, the transformations are remarkable. "Before I went to a vipassana meditation . . . I was probably the angriest man in this prison," said a convicted murderer named Grady Bankhead, who came within hours of being executed before his sentence was reduced to life imprisonment and he was moved off death row. He had reason to be angry. When Bankhead was three years old, his mother left him and his little brother in a farmhouse, telling them she would be back soon. He didn't see her again until he landed on death row. In the meantime, his brother had died. Meditation helped Bankhead get to the root of his anger. Now he's recruiting other inmates to take the challenging course. "We have to have some kind of balance back in our lives from the horrible things that we've done," Bankhead said. Another inmate agreed: "Meditation changed my life."

Like the meditating inmates, we can come to understand that we don't have to live beset by constant turbulence and anxiety and regret. We may be incarcerated in a prison of our own making, but we can spring the lock and live in greater peace and serenity and joy.

The practice of compassion reminds us that we are larger than our anger, our misfortune, and even our pain. Because we have suffered, we want to make this a better world, and we can act without timidity or equivocation. Our vision of life can become vast, fueled by compelling moral force.

Several years ago, I met Myles Horton, who founded the Highlander Folk School, a training center for civil rights activists. (Rosa Parks attended a course there a few months before her historic bus ride.) Myles asked me what I did, and when I mentioned lovingkindness meditation, he said, "Oh, Marty [Martin Luther King, Jr.] used to say to me, 'You have to love everybody.' And I would say, 'No, I don't. I'm only going to love the people that deserve to be loved.' And Marty would laugh and say, 'No, no, no, you have to love everybody.'"

When Myles told that story to people, they would sometimes say, "Well, look what happened: King was assassinated"—as if this were a case of cause and effect, and King would not have been killed if he hadn't tried to love everybody. But do we really believe that if Martin Luther King, Jr., had been vicious and small-minded and full of hate, he would have been protected from harm?

Insightful Patience

Once you have developed a level of tolerant patience through cultivating endurance, you can mobilize your analytical mindfulness to take it further, into the territory of active forbearance based on the realistic insight of critical wisdom. Anger always burns within a framework, a conceptual targeting that springs from the habitual, even instinctive constricting of the self and pushing away of the other. When we are angry with someone, the relationship becomes Us-versus-Them. We no longer see the person as an individual like us, with feelings and needs like ours, but we regard them solely in terms of how they affect us. We become all-consumed with the enemy's intentions, projecting on to them our own ruthless, malevolent intentions to harm. Then we become paranoid about what the enemy might do, and our anger explodes preemptively as we desperately struggle to remove the threat.

We can see, then, that anger, while seeming to be a naturally occurring force, actually operates within a very specific habitual framework. Our choice of that particular person as an enemy is based on our perception of that person as someone who quite deliberately has chosen, is choosing, or will choose to harm us. However, when we bring a more focused mindfulness to the situation and analyze ourselves, our enemy, and the situation, we can see that the enemy's behavior is driven by their own unconscious impulses and attitudes, just as our own behavior is driven by ours. Both of us are victims of our inner drives.

Just as bacteria and viruses and chemical pollutants produce diseases in your body without having any conscious intention to do so, so an unaware person is driven to emotional anger by their mental addictions—delusion, lust, hatred, envy, and so on—which are all operating unconsciously, without intent. People under the spell of the anger addiction do not will themselves to manifest anger: they simply freak out and explode. Sometimes, while you still have freedom of choice in a situation, you might think, *I should get angry with this or that, but I won't,* so there is always a bit of room to change course before you explode. But once you give in to it, the very nature of anger is that it takes hold of you and deprives you of free will and intelligent choice. When anger arises and transforms into rage and fury, it does so without any free agency. Just as fire does not choose to burn a log but does so automatically, you and your anger, and your enemy and his or her anger, operate without voluntary intent. So there is no one to blame, except the process of anger itself.

The same is true of all negative mental habits, such as lust, envy, and arrogance. Once you develop insight into the mechanical nature of these inner processes, your inwardly critical mindfulness can penetrate to the level of liberating insight. You can see through the notion of conscious choice in other people's destructive emotions and unskillful actions. That awareness enables you to break free from your mental addictions to anger and hatred, and rise to a vision of the world as a network of impersonal causes and conditions.

This network of interconnection lacks any personality, any identifiable free agency that intends you harm, so there is no real target for your anger that you can point to as the source of your suffering. You begin to see that anger toward your so-called enemies is unrealistic. You have nothing to gain by destroying your enemy. In broadening your vision of the causal network of conditions, you begin to find a plane of freedom from it, baby step by baby step.

But something else is at work here as well. What about *my* self and the self of my enemy, the one who does me wrong? There seems to be a clearly identifiable "me," so we naturally assume an independent self in the enemy. But even a casual examination within is disappointing. We cannot find our "self" when we look for it. Is it in the brain? A particular neuron? In the heart? If the heart, in which part? The muscle around it? One of the chambers? The more we look, the more elusive the self seems. And when we see that, our certainty erodes. We become less sure of the malevolent intent of our enemies and see them as the victims of conditions.

Religious and philosophical arguments for the existence of the "immortal soul" or "essential self" tend to present it as an absolute entity intrinsically beyond the relative world. By definition such a soul is irreducible, unchanging, and nonrelational—suprahuman—and therefore both Eastern and Western critical analysts (Buddhist mind scientists and modern neuroscientists) argue that such an absolute entity cannot rationally be considered a thinking or acting agent that relates to other agents and circumstances. Modern scientists infer from this that there is no such thing as a soul, and no former and future lives of individual beings, thus confirming their philosophical materialism. Buddhist mind scientists vary in their theories, some simply substituting a constantly changing continuum (Sanskrit *samtana*) for a soul, and the most advanced ones allowing a constantly changing continuum called a "super-subtle indestructible drop" (Sanskrit, *sukshma-anakshara-bindu*) to serve as the carrier of evolved traits from life to life.

This discussion of the self and its levels and layers could be advanced further by using the sophisticated investigations and critical metaphysical reasoning developed in the Buddhist monastic universities of India and Tibet, but for our purposes here it is enough to say that, according to the mind science tradition of India and Tibet, a permanent, absolute (nonrelational), unchanging entity called a "soul" or "self" or "identity" cannot be found; our belief that we have a fixed identity is an illusion. Obviously, an illusion cannot participate in relational, conditional processes of action—thinking, speaking, or moving physically. Shantideva argues that if the self were permanent (as claimed by some schools of Indian thought), it would be incapable of doing anything, since how could it act without changing itself? The absurd consequence, he points out, is that even empty space would then have to be considered a "self," since space is clearly unchanging and inactive.

Our critical insight into the reality of the enemy's lack of an absolute self capable of conscious agency empowers our patience by critically releasing our perceptions from concretizing an entire structure within which anger can control us, one built on the "real self" of the enemy, his conscious harm, and our real need for revenge. But all these are simply ideas that emerge in our experiential awareness as constructs of our mental habits. No longer must we endure the whole drama of harm and revenge enacted between our "self" and the "self" of our enemy. As we see through their supposed objectivity, we are able to break free from the imagined inevitability of what is happening and what we must do about it. And as our fixated certainty about the enemy's intent and our state of being wronged becomes more fluid, we reach a different level of resilience and flexibility in how we respond. Where before we felt we had no choice but to be furiously angry about what was surely too much to bear, now we can be patient and more careful about what we perceive and how we respond, since we are able to see external circumstances and our own internal mind-states from many different angles. Once we no longer objectify our perceptions, when we see something going wrong or being different from the way we want it, we can take it with a grain of salt—not let it get to us and increase our frustration—or we can take appropriate action.

By developing the patience born of insight, we can prevent frustration over things not going our way from bursting into anger. We can remain cheerful by reflecting on the conditionality of all things—that they happen automatically when conditions become ripe for various causes (such as our own past actions) to produce their effects. We no longer have to interpret people and situations as inevitable enemies; we can engage with them calmly and cooly to shift their course from negative to positive.

Ultimately, nobody wants to suffer—not us, not our friend, not our enemy. If people always made rational choices, no one would ever suffer. But as long as we are in thrall to our anger, we will continue to create the causes that lead to effects in our lives that are the very opposite of what we desire.

As you free yourself from your anger addiction, you can begin to see how helpless all beings are, even your enemies. You realize how suffering only comes about because of the confusion and mental addictions that human beings are caught in, which deprive us of any freedom of choice or will. It might be hard to feel compassion right away for someone who is trying to harm you. Understandably, you may be gripped by fight-or-flight reactions. And practically speaking, you may need to defend yourself, so you may have no time to feel for your attacker. But why bother to explode in anger? Save your energy for coming up with the most effective, rational response you can think of to avoid the harm, or for finding the most efficient means of cooling down the enemy.

Now that you know that your enemy is merely the tool of his own anger, you can be angry only with the mental addiction that drives him. You can be angry with his anger, with anger itself. Your anger at anger effectively becomes the energy of tolerance.

HEALING THROUGH ADVERSITY

In a time of despair, when I felt disconnected from all that was good in my life, I was helped a lot by something Rilke wrote to comfort a troubled young man in *Letters to a Young Poet:* "So you mustn't be frightened . . . if a sadness rises in front of you, larger than any you have ever seen. . . . You must realize . . . that life has not forgotten you. . . ."[7]

A sense of having been forgotten by "normal" life is common when we are going through difficult times, as if we are trapped in a parallel universe where broken people live. But when we realize that healing can spring from the deepest sorrow, we regain our connection with the suffering world and trust that we can reenter the "unbroken" zone. Awareness of connection creates the path for transforming suffering into positive change. We do not seek pain, of course; but when it happens—and it will—we learn to bear it differently, as an unavoidable part of being alive, a shared struggle that joins us to our brothers and sisters, rather than as a

---

7   Rainer Maria Rilke, *Letters to a Young Poet,* trans. Stephen Mitchell (New York: Modern Library, 2001), pp. 92–93.

relentless problem we can never seem to fix, an enemy we cannot hope to conquer.

It is possible to metabolize grief in ways that don't produce hostility but that nourish our lives, our families, and our communities, and offer lessons for moral and spiritual growth. We see that freedom depends on our ability to open to a bigger context. In the midst of pain, we look toward what is whole and undamaged.

It is not that everything becomes all right; but everything is recognized as part of the immense story of life, of nature, of truth. It's certainly not that everything becomes pleasant or inconsequential; but we are no longer defined by trauma, because now we have a more powerful sense of wholeness and connection.

In late September 2001, I was leading a meditation workshop in New York. One of the participants told the class, "I am a fireman." In that moment, in that town, we all knew exactly what his statement implied. After a pause, he went on, "The towers collapsed on top of me. I escaped, though many of my friends did not. I decided that I didn't want my life to end there. I wanted to find a way to go on."

Not only did he go on, but he helped many people through their own darkness. This firefighter and I became good friends. The last time I saw him was at a program I taught near the World Trade Center site as part of a commemoration of the tenth anniversary of 9/11. I was surprised that the firefighter had been willing to be in the immediate area of ground zero so close to the anniversary, but I was very touched that he had. When I told him that, he spoke of how important it felt to him to see new buildings going up on that site—that it had ripped him apart to face that jagged hole in the ground. He needed to see that life had gone on.

Forgiving Patience

The third kind of patience we need to develop is forgiving patience, the most advanced patience. To gain full freedom from involuntary anger and hatred, we must reach the point where we can forgive anyone who harms us, no matter in what way. When anything bad happens to us, our most effective move is to go after the source as if it lies within ourselves. Sitting and blaming others will do no good; that only strengthens our sense of helplessness, since we cannot control others, only ourselves.

Paradoxically, then, in order to overcome being the victim, we can skillfully, joyfully, blame ourselves. Contrary to conventional thinking, blaming the victim when the victim is yourself does not deepen your victimization; on the contrary, it sets you on the path of freeing yourself from victimization. When you take responsibility for what happens to you, you take command of it. You reason to yourself like this: *Okay, I was harmed. I often harm others, I must have harmed others in the past, and so now I am being harmed in turn. How excellent that I am getting rid of that evolutionary consequence! Now I will never harm those beings again, so I will not be harmed. I will avoid the consequences of other past harm I committed. And I will help others so that energetically it will outweigh any harm I must have caused.*

We can look at our past and present behavior and recognize how self-centered and stubbornly unenlightened we have been. We habitually try to run away from suffering and toward the slightest external happiness, fleeting though it may turn out to be. We are addicted to pleasure, and we thirst for it, while being in denial that we constantly feel dissatisfied with what we get. We are addicted to anger as a means of removing obstacles to our desires; and, in following the dictates of our anger, we are driven to self-destruction.

We can now take responsibility for the enemies who torment us, since hurting us is their involuntary reaction to their fear that we will harm them or their subliminal memory of our having hurt them in the evolutionary past. So not only should we not be angry with them, but we should feel remorse that we affected them so negatively in the past and caused them to live in such pain. Here we begin to enter the realm of patience as active forgiveness. Joyfully, ecstatically, we celebrate our initial freedom from fear of suffering by going beyond patience as tolerant endurance and patience as insightful forbearance, to experience patience as nonretaliation and forgiveness. Such active forgiveness opens the golden door of the exalting temple of universal compassion, which is the amazing realm of realistic happiness and natural bliss.

So our enemies provide us with irritation, injury, and harm, which are the occasions for us to practice endurance, forbearance, and forgiveness. The worse they treat us, the more we benefit. We can even see that at the same time our enemies are harming us, we are harming them by allowing them to mistreat us, for the consequence of their harmful acts will be a miserable future for them.

Given the benefits of suffering, we might conclude that harming our enemies in retaliation would actually help them by giving *them* a chance to practice patience. As tempting as this rationalization is, the reality is that unless our enemies know how to practice patience, harm and suffering will only make them angrier, increasing the likelihood that they will do more bad things, thereby making their downward spiral even greater.

In learning to be patient no matter what anyone does to us, it is critical to remember that even though our physical bodies can suffer greatly, no outside aggression can harm the subtle body-mind that in its essence is a continuum of joyful bliss. As you are working on developing patience, it helps to understand that it is your "coarse mind," which functions at the level of senses and personality, that is holding your body hostage, tormenting it and plunging it back into your anger addiction. We need to learn to sometimes disidentify from our coarse minds and bodies in order to develop the deepest, pain-defying level of patience and immunity to anger. We can of course only do this when we have grown free of the fear of death, by having carefully and thoroughly examined the realities of the process of life and death in both intellectual and experiential ways.

RIGHT SPEECH

Human interaction is seldom simple. One of the biggest problems we encounter is verbal communication that is misunderstood or unskillfully handled. That is why the Buddha, in describing how to live in harmony with one another, put great emphasis on what he called "right speech."

How we communicate has everything to do with maintaining harmony and well-being. Communication between adversaries easily devolves into brutal he-said-she-said exchanges. The criteria the Buddha used for determining right speech were simple: *Is it true? Is it useful?* When he urged people to speak the truth, he obviously did not mean that we should say whatever we think, however brash or hurtful it might be. Sensitivity and discernment are essential. Saying what is true and what is useful requires mindfulness.

Even during conflict, it is remarkable how differently we relate to others when we respond from a place of awareness. My student Elizabeth described how a shift of perspective changed her interactions with others. It began with her shouting at her husband, "Are you calling me a liar?" Elizabeth and her husband were arguing because Elizabeth needed her husband to give her a ride to and from her optometrist's office, but her eye appointment conflicted with her husband's schedule. If Elizabeth canceled the appointment, she feared it would be a month before she could reschedule. When she reminded her husband that the appointment had been on their calendar for the past three months, he said coldly, "Well, if it was there, I would have noticed it." That's when Elizabeth lost it: how dare he call her a liar! Upon hearing her angry words, he turned and stormed away.

It was a familiar pattern, Elizabeth said: a perceived putdown followed by an overreaction as each tried to prove being right or one of them stormed away. Every fight, she said, left them with "a sting in the heart." Then one night in her meditation, the words *Nothing matters* suddenly popped into her head. Immediately, she felt freer. A few days later, after a contentious phone call with her son, she meditated on the phrase *Nothing matters.* Again, her tension melted. But this time, *Nothing matters* was followed by the words *And it's only because nothing matters that everything matters.* That really gave her something to think about.

She still gets angry, Elizabeth said, but "when I make time to meditate, repeating *Nothing matters* as a mantra, while staying aware of the truth that everything matters, my heart gradually gives up the need to be right. And the sting dissolves, both out there (with her husband) and in here." Elizabeth's story demonstrates her realization that she need not say anything in retaliation when she gets angry. At times, being silent is better than speech that is not true or useful.

One way of restating the paradox Elizabeth discovered is to ask yourself: *What actually matters most at this moment? What do I really care about more than anything else right now?* Elizabeth's story raises an important point: When you find yourself in conflict, do you care more about being right or being happy? Can you step down off your pedestal long enough to acknowledge that being right might not matter if it only prolongs suffering?

Another friend of mine has a wonderful saying about

getting older: *More happens, less matters.* This is akin to Elizabeth's insight that nothing matters if it brings fleeting or shallow satisfaction yet perpetuates ongoing conflict and pain. But because, in a broader, spiritual sense, everything matters, nothing in our conflicts matters *enough* to merit the suffering we inflict on ourselves and others.

Words That Hurt

When we are harmed on the verbal level, the pain is not physical, but it can be a powerful cause of anger. We often take strong offense and become highly indignant when an insult or slander or abusive speech is directed at us. Yet it is essential to realize that speech causes us emotional pain only when we let it arouse us.

You don't want others to think badly of you? Then don't get angry at their insults or harsh words. If you ignore attempts to provoke you, maintaining good cheer in spite of others' hostility, even such people will run out of excuses for disliking you. Perhaps, however, you think you will suffer loss of reputation and even loss of income if you ignore the bad things people say about you. But being angry will not ensure your reputation or restore your income; often, in fact, it will make your situation worse. You have a far better chance of defending your reputation and livelihood if you stay cool and act strategically.

True integrity can arise only when we decide that indulging in angry outbursts or bouts of negative action would be a fate worse than anything, even injury or death. We must be determined to keep that vow no matter what.

Here you really need to think about the quality of your life. Conquering the inner enemy requires that you have enough concern about your impact on others to live in a way that goes beyond your habitual self-concern. The energy you invest in restraining your anger must be more powerful than your concern for your immediate goals.

We seem not to mind criticism as long as it's directed at someone else. When we are the target, it's a different matter. But when we are criticized, it's because we have been greedy, angry, proud, stingy, prejudiced, or deluded, so in reality, the criticism is directed at these mental addictions. Because we are so closely identified with our mental addictions, getting rid of them can be very difficult. The key here is to develop mindfulness, a subtle awareness of the many strands of your relative self—your actual, ever-changing self that is free of any supposed fixed, independent, absolute self—so that you can disidentify with the strands you would rather jettison (your inner enemies) just as would disassociate yourself from a person who was harming you.

Whenever something harmful happens to you, you can employ the patience of insight to see the reality of the situation. Delusion is to blame. Both the person who harmed you verbally in anger and you who responded in kind fail to see that expressing anger in words can be every bit as harmful as inflicting physical injury. You may think of yourself as innocent, attacked unreasonably by your enemy and therefore argue that your anger is not as bad as the harm your enemy inflicted. However, if you consider that the deeper cause of his harming you may be your own harmful actions and anger toward him on previous occasions—or in previous existences—this levels the field and calms your righteous indignation, a major fuel of explosive anger. You come to realize that the only way to break the vicious circle of harm—you harm him, he harms you—is to refrain from blowing up and instead convert that white-hot energy into the fierce determination to sustain forbearance. In this way, you give the immediate moment, which gives you the choice between habitual reaction and mindful nonreaction, infinite significance by being conscious of its link to the endless chain of consequences that constitutes the continuous relativity of life.

Once you open the moment to its infinite dimension, your mindfulness intensifies in its scope and power, and the strength comes through you to turn your attention in a positive direction. Initially, your focus is on your own positivity, but soon you will recognize that you can model positivity for others as the way to happiness. The vicious circle of endless mutual harm turns into a virtuous circle of endless mutual benefit, powered by patience, forbearance, and love.

Shantideva uses a strong analogy to bring into focus the power of shifting to the infinity perspective: Imagine you are a criminal sentenced to death for some heinous crime, and on the verge of your execution the king intervenes and orders the executioner to chop off your left pinkie instead of your head. Although the pain of the injured hand is agonizing, it is mixed with joy and relief because your life has been spared. In the same way, when you realize the infinite danger of giving way to hatred and anger in reaction to some injury done to you, you experience the infinite benefit of restraining your reaction and instead expressing patience, kindness, and compassion. You can then receive the harm without losing your joyfulness, because you are ending a cycle of violence.

If your mind complains bitterly at how painful it is to refrain from retaliating, you can use your discomfort to intensify your awareness of how much worse the pain would be if you gave in to hatred and dealt out more harm to the other person. Any situation can always get worse; you can never assume that something is as bad as it can get. To the question "What does it matter if I lose my temper?" the answer is, it always matters—and in the infinite evolutionary perspective, the tiniest thing, bad or good, matters infinitely. This profound expansion of your mindful awareness of the moment leads to a sort of joy even in suffering, since your mind interprets the pain as the doorway to a higher freedom from pain, for others as well as yourself.

Addiction to Jealousy

Anger has a close cousin and ally in jealousy. The antidote to jealousy is what Buddhist psychology calls "sympathetic" or "congratulatory" joy. I think of it as jubilation or rejoicing in the good fortune of others. One of my Tibetan Buddhist teachers called such joy the lazy person's way to accumulate merit and make progress toward enlightenment. Someone else does something truly great with heroic effort, and you forego a knee-jerk attack of envy and instead sincerely rejoice in her success, thereby you earn some of the merit for yourself with very little effort. Of course, by the same token, you have to be careful not to let your mind carelessly indulge in perverse pleasure when someone else does something truly bad—like relishing someone's well-planned bank robbery—since that earns you a share of karmic demerit. When a rival receives praise, you lose doubly if you give in to envy; not only do you not receive the praise; but, on top of that, your disgruntlement makes you even unhappier.

PRAISE AND BLAME

I gave a talk recently; and, at the end, I was surrounded by people coming up to thank me, saying how much benefit they had gotten from what I'd said. Of course, it was terrific to receive so much praise. The next morning I met with the person who had organized the lecture. As we sat and drank tea, she told me that she had run into someone who had been at the lecture the night before, a woman who had, in fact, come to every single lecture in the series, and she didn't like any of them. When she asked this woman what she thought of my talk, true to course, the woman replied that she had disliked it. "Any aspect in particular?" the organizer asked. "Oh," the woman replied, "the contents." In other words, everything!

This is how it is in the world of pleasure and pain, gain and loss, praise and blame, fame and disrepute. We are forever being pulled and pushed by shifting feedback from the outside world. We yearn for pleasure, gain, praise, and fame, and feel resentful when instead we get pain, loss, blame, or disrepute. As human beings, it is inevitable that we will have some response to praise and blame, but it is equally inevitable that we will live through many opposites of experience in our lifetime, and this fact of duality need not be our enemy.

There's a story about this alternation of opposites in the Buddhist teachings:

A man went to a monastery one day to learn something of the Buddha's message. The first person he came upon was a monk who had taken a temporary vow of silence. When the visitor asked the monk to tell him something about the Buddha's teachings, the monk remained silent. That infuriated the visitor, who stomped away. On the second day, the man returned and came upon a disciple of the Buddha who was famous not only for his profound personal realization but also for his vast theoretical knowledge. When asked to describe some of the Buddha's teaching, he launched into a lengthy discourse that likewise infuriated the visitor, who again stomped away.

On the third day, the man returned and encountered yet another disciple of the Buddha, who, having heard what happened on the first and second days, was careful to say a little bit but not too much. Once again the man became angry, shouting, "How dare you treat such profound matters so sketchily!" before stomping away.

Finally, the disciples who had aroused the man's ire went off to see the Buddha and recounted the story. You can imagine the Buddha's amusement over their consternation. "There is always blame in this world," he told them. "If you say nothing, they will blame you. If you say too much, they will blame you. There is always blame in this world."

In other words, we cannot always rely on being given the esteem of others. If we are counting on a changeable world, outside of our dominion or control, to give us a feeling of self-worth, we're in trouble. That doesn't mean we don't care what others think. Of course we care. We want to be thanked for our generosity, noticed for our courage, appreciated for our strengths and virtue. We would all rather be adored than scorned. This is human nature. But the question is, how much do we care? From where do we draw our sense of integrity? What is the source of our conviction and our willingness to take a risk? From where do we summon the strength to be a little different, or express ourselves, or step forward, or just be ourselves? If I am only happy when universally praised and adored, and cannot be happy if there is any hint of disagreement or criticism coming my way, I will not be content for long.

By shifting our relationship to praise and blame, we free ourselves from the habit of interjecting the opinions and prejudices of others. We can weigh the truthfulness of feedback instead of automatically discounting negative opinions. Fielding criticism with an open mind, we can learn from dissent. Regardless of how perfect we think we are, there will always be someone who sees our warts. Until we temper our reactions with wisdom, we will continue to feel antagonized by our lack of control over others' views.

Not long ago, I had another lesson in praise and blame. I was in Washington, D.C., sitting with a friend in an auditorium, waiting for the speaker to begin. I spotted a woman carrying my book *Faith*, with its distinctive saffron-colored cover. "Look, she has *Faith*," I said to my friend. At that point the woman saw me and came over so

I could sign the book. As she was leaving, she said to me, "You are a goddess." I was embarrassed but also pretty happy she'd said that.

Not one minute later, someone brought over a journalist to meet me. I'd say that of all the people I've encountered in my life, he ranked close to being the least interested in an introduction to me. The go-between said, "This is Sharon Salzberg. Have you ever heard of her?" Looking totally bored, the journalist replied, "Nah!" My friend then whispered to me, "Tell him you're a goddess."

Yeah, right. It hadn't taken me even a minute to plunge from goddess status to being of no interest at all! In the end, peace comes from realizing that while we can try to be kind and bring gladness to others, we cannot determine everyone's reactions. Or anyone's really.

There is a story about the Buddha that points to such wisdom. One day, the Buddha was walking across a plot of land when a man came up and angrily started shaking his fist in the Buddha's face, saying he had no right to be walking there. The Buddha looked at the man and said, "Tell me, if you prepared a lovely gift for someone, and you reached out to give it to them but they refused to accept it, to whom would the gift belong?" "To me, of course," the man replied. "Just so," the Buddha said. "I'm not accepting the gift of your anger. Therefore, it remains with you."

To sense which gifts to accept and which to leave behind is our path to discovering freedom.

A craving for praise and fame in themselves can become every bit as addictive as anger, an inner enemy that distracts us from pursuing what is truly meaningful in our lives. Seeming to be an advantage, accolades can deflect our attention from our inner growth and spiritual practice. The enemies, who seek to destroy our reputation by gossiping or lying about us, or exaggerating our negative qualities, actually help us to avoid distractions and stick to the main focus of life. So from my own selfish perspective, I should treasure my enemies!

One of my most humorous and creative teachers, Tara Tulku, really shocked me at one point. After I had been practicing Buddhism for years and thinking I had made some progress, he said that if I really knew what I was doing in this lifetime, I would be happier to come down for breakfast in the morning and meet my worst enemy at the door than I would be to greet a TV prize-show host ringing the doorbell and presenting me with a check for $10 million. I had to admit I was still far from attaining that perspective. His point, of course, is that we should treasure our enemies and use their harm to develop transcendent patience. Given the tenacity of inner enemies, most of us will have plenty of opportunities to follow his advice.

The Dalai Lama's long decades of meditation on Mao Zedong, the great enemy of Tibet and its people, perfectly exemplifies this. Asked once who in the world he most admired, the Dalai Lama mentioned Gandhi, the apostle of nonviolence, and then, to everyone's surprise, Chairman Mao, an apostle of violence and the destroyer of Tibetan freedom, along with its monasteries, its environment, and over a million of its people. Was this admiration going too far, I wondered—a carryover from the Dalai Lama's meditation on appreciating his enemies for giving him the opportunity to practice compassion? Was it even a trifle self-serving, focusing on the patience he could extract from the harm done to Tibet, rather than on the need to save Mao from the negative effects of his destructive actions? I'm sure it was neither of these, but some very deep vision of Mao's inner being that His Holiness could still admire, even though he is perfectly aware that Mao caused immeasurable harm to so many beings. Such a vision is still beyond me, but I have a tiny intuition that it is there, in the infinite compassion of Avalokiteshvara, the Bodhisattva of Compassion, who represents the infinite altruism of enlightened beings and who is incarnated in the Dalai Lamas.

Our enemies provide an opportunity to practice patient tolerance of the intolerant. Here is love returned for hate, good for evil. This is the realm of all great spiritual beings, the saints and adepts from every tradition throughout history.

Once, when I was giving a talk on patience, someone asked me, "So where are all these heroes of patience today, on our violent, strife-filled planet?" For a moment I was at a loss how to respond, and I was about to reply, rather meekly, "They're there, but we just don't see them." Then a memory suddenly flashed through my mind of a row I had had with one of my sons that was similar to rows in my youth between my brothers and me, and sometimes even with our father. Both then and now, it was the woman of the family—my mother and later my wife—who intervened to calm the rage, putting herself between the loud voices and raised fists. So in a flash of inspiration I said, "The women are the heroes who get in the way of the harsh words and the angry blows, who appeal to our better angels and calm the furies. They are the cool heroes." I have become more and more convinced of this as I look around the world and back through history. This is not to say that women are the only people attempting to maintain peace today, but in the public arena as well as at home, they continue to be the ones seeking ways to create harmony without using threats or force.

The Buddha's insight was that every individual's existence is interdependent with every other individual's. So making all our interactions positive ones—asserting ourselves with generosity and fairness, and receiving the assertions of others with patience and tolerance—is mutually beneficial. Altruism, which is grounded in our sense of identification with others and reinforced by the idea that we have a moral obligation to help them, is actually enlightened self-interest.

We have spoken of a bodhisattva as a person with a long-term, heartfelt dedication to helping other beings find happiness. The vicious circle of enmity and injury ends when a bodhisattva does not respond to harm in kind but instead embraces the harmer with patience, acceptance, forgiveness, and love. The Buddha treated all beings as equals, worthy of respect, enemies included. Never mind that his enemies were always trying to do him in. He never held it against them, and some of his fiercest enemies went on to become his most dedicated followers.

If we treated our enemies as if they were Buddha or Jesus, we would be far less likely to lose patience with them. We do not need to invite enemies to harm us, and we need not passively submit to it when they do. But whenever our inner enemies of anger, hatred, jealousy, and their other cousins attack us, we can use it as an opportunity to practice patience with ourselves, as we do whatever it takes to overcome destructive emotions.

The insight of patience is that our enemy, outer or inner, is our opportunity to awaken. Through the yoga of patience we overcome the inner enemy of anger and hatred, transforming our relationships with our outer enemies in the process.

THE MYTH OF CONTROL

One of the reasons we judge ourselves harshly is our belief that we ought to have far greater control over outcomes in life than we do. We tend to label as "enemy" what we cannot control, whether externally—people or situations— or internally, namely our thoughts and emotions. Only when we begin to question the assumption that what lies outside our control is our adversary can we stop making enemies of others and ourselves.

The key to exploding the myth of control is recognizing the truths of interconnection and impermanence. The Buddha taught that nothing exists independently of the causes and conditions that bring it about. If certain conversations, interactions, and events had not occurred, you would not be sitting here at this moment reading this book. As parts of a greater whole, we do not orchestrate the grand motion of the universe. We have a measure of control over our own behavior on a good day, but beyond that our powers are pretty limited. To a self-preoccupied eye, we are fundamentally isolated and alone, seeking connection only out of a futile reach for control. But to an eye attuned to interdependence, everything exists in a web or network of relationships.

And because of conditionality, nothing is rigid, impermeable, or fixed. We can let go of our divisive strategies, contrivances, and obsessive efforts to control and recognize how fluid life is. Seasons change. Things move. People transform. Situations shift. We live in a world where no matter what, that's going to be the reality. Every aspect of life—including healing—has its own rhythm, its own flow, and its own movement, and we cannot dictate the rate of that change. We can respond to this truth with resistance or with wisdom. Perceiving ourselves as part of an immense reality of change connects us to all of life. Once we dispel the illusion of being separate and static, we work with change instead of against it, and we no longer feel the need to brandish a closed fist at the world.

There are many things we can know, and many things we cannot. It is in the place between the known and the unknown that we find these essential truths. We can't know how something will end, or whether someone will recover from an illness, or when or how we will die, but we can know that we all will die. We can't know what thought will arise next in our minds, but we can know it will be impermanent, evanescent. We can't know if a relationship will last, but we can know that vengefulness brings suffering and lovingkindness brings happiness. We can't know the result of an action, but we can know that our actions have consequences, because we are all interconnected.

We can't even know what the next breath will feel like, but we know that our life hangs upon this delicate movement of air. We can't necessarily know the outcome of a job interview, but we can know that everything in this universe that has the nature to arise also has the nature to pass away. We can't know what will happen tomorrow, but we can know that one thing leads to the next.

We can know that all experiences are impermanent and interconnected, and that they exist only because of the conditions that bring them about and in no way apart from those. We may not comprehend why there is so much suffering in this world, why some people behave so badly toward others; but we can know, as the Buddha said, that hatred will never cease by hatred—it will only cease by love. We can't know what the future holds; but we can know where happiness, strength, and wisdom are to be found. We can feel the rhythm of these truths underneath the ordinary flow of events as surely as we can feel the rhythm of the surf when we're sitting on the shore. Even in this world of constant change and uncertainty that we cannot control, we can be free of enmity and fear.

BEFRIENDING
TIME

Whatever has the power to hurt, anger, or disappoint us by diminishing or disappearing will be perceived as an enemy. Turning time into an idol, a coveted object we long to possess, makes life a losing battle. Greediness for more time automatically creates an atmosphere of tension and dread. The minute time becomes a commodity, we make it not only ours to lose but also ours to judge. I have often looked back over a meditation session and asked myself, "Was that a good one or a bad one?" But like any life experience, the meditation session was never just one thing: there were moments of peace, moments of anger, moments of joy, moments of sadness, moments of sleepiness, moments of energy. Our movement through time is constantly changing, but we tend to lump all the moments together and respond to time as if it were one thing.

We indulge in the same magical thinking regarding the future, collapsing our imagined future experience into one dimension ("This painful feeling is going to be here forever") that we then cling to or reject. We do everything we can to master time—to make sure that everything stays the way we want it or that whatever is distasteful changes immediately. But time is a dance-away lover. Trying to bend it to our wishes, we live out of sync with the present moment and in defiance of the laws of nature.

When I first went to India as a meditation student, I was so happy that I planned to stay there for the rest of my life. It was inconceivable to me that I would live anywhere else. Because of that certainty, whenever I sat down to meditate, I found myself obsessing over my visa. In those days, it was very difficult to get an extended visa, so day after day I would sit there on my cushion, mapping out my strategy for extending mine. *Okay, next year when I need a visa extension, I'll go to that town because it's very close and they're bound to give me a visa. The year after that, I'll go to this other place because it's really remote and no one goes there, so getting the visa should be a snap. And then, the year after that when I need a visa extension, I'll go to this other city because I heard those people are really corrupt and I can bribe them. Then the year after that . . .* Suddenly, the bell would ring and that would be the end of my sitting. When the next sitting began, I would begin the same thing all over again because I wanted to stay in India so much.

Clearly I needed to stop trying to control the future with my obsession. I discovered two very helpful tools in my efforts to do this. The first was to ask myself, *What are you feeling right now?* Asking this question enabled me to get in touch with the basic anxiety—*Will I be able to get what I want?*—and the core yearning underneath the travelogue of India. The second tool was counsel I gave myself: *You're not really in India while you're India, because all you're doing is planning how to be able to stay in India. Why not be in India while you're in India?* This reminder was crucial, because as things turned out, I obviously did not end up staying in India for the rest of my life.

This is how mindfulness can heal our relationship with time. Seeing our tendency to lean forward into the future or rehash issues in the past, we learn to bring our attention and energy back to the present and connect with what's actually happening in this moment. We can also choose whether to frame uncertainty about the future in positive or negative terms. Do you expect only the worst, or do you remain open to the possibility of marvelous things to come? Do you see the world through dread-inducing eyes or through a lens of eager anticipation and curiosity?

The flip side of dread is impatience, another attempt to control time's passage. We often feel as if we don't have enough time, that time is running out, so we struggle to fill every moment. Fearful of wasting a second, we hoard time as if it were money. This creates an underlying sense of panic in our busy lives. Contemplating the passage of time, we are filled with disbelief. (When I think that 40 years have gone by since I first went to India, it is unbelievable to me!) We feel sorrow about the passage of time and fear of not using it optimally before it's too late. Because as we age we have less time left before we die than we once did, we turn nature's most intractable process into a form of personal larceny, and its passage becomes our biggest problem. This creates ambivalence toward the organic unfolding of life and the natural rhythm of how things are.

Our culture does little to teach us patience or acceptance of time's passing. Bombardment by the slogans of late-night TV pitchmen is enough to scare a time-fearing person to death: *Act now! You must call in the next 15 minutes!*

Our relationship to time warps in both directions: when circumstances are pleasant, we want it to stop; and when times are bad, we try to push the fast-forward button. We're trained to keep our eyes on the future and remember the past (in order not to repeat it), thus situating our minds anywhere but here. In our youth-obsessed, age-phobic, death-denying, planned-obsolescence, cyber-fast culture, the goal is to cheat time at every opportunity and bend it to our wishes. Technology actually negates time (or tries to), giving us the ability to connect instantly and simultaneously to an array of information, sources, people, and places. In this rapid-fire information age, impatience is rewarded while delayed gratification is considered passé. Recently, I was at a retreat center that had only dial-up Internet service. (Imagine!) Being forced to wait for dial-up to connect nearly ruined my day.

Years ago, I went to see a beloved Tibetan teacher, the late Nyoshul Khen Rinpoche, in Taiwan. After the visit, my traveling companions and I planned to see Rinpoche again in a few days. But during the interim he had moved somewhere else. A group of us, holding flowers and offerings, were waiting outside our hotel for taxis to take us to the new place. I was feeling incredibly sad. When we had visited Rinpoche, he had seemed especially frail and ill. And now all I could think was, *Oh, no, this could be the last time I ever see him.* The prospect was devastating, and I was deeply upset.

After the taxis picked us up, they got completely lost in the streets of Taiwan. In that moment, my attitude toward seeing Rinpoche suddenly shifted. Elated, I started thinking, *I'd give anything to see him one more time. One more time would be the best thing in the entire universe! It would be the greatest gift I could ever have!*

As it turned out, the taxis eventually found the right address, and we were able to see Rinpoche. Contrary to what I feared, he lived many more years, and I saw him many more times. But that experience taught me a valuable lesson, as I saw clearly how "one more time" can be the best prospect imaginable or the worst, depending on how I relate to it.

The feeling of being chased by the shadow of time creates untold suffering in our lives. That's why I tell students, if you feel like there's never enough time to do all things you need to do, maybe you need to do fewer things. I love what the theologian Howard Thurman said: "Don't ask what the world needs. Ask what makes you come alive and go do it, because what the world needs is people who have come alive."[8]

Philosophers and physicists have told us that there are two kinds of time operating in the world: manmade time and cosmic time. It is critical that we pay attention to both if we hope to maintain any kind of balance. The ancients had a name for hourglass time—*nunc fluens* (Latin for "flowing now")—the metronomic, tick-tocking of chronological time that frays your nerves, grays your hair, and forms rings inside the trunk of a tree. And then there is *nunc stans* ("abiding now"), time as viewed through the fullness of the present moment.

---

8   Quoted at The Howard Thurman Center for Common Ground, www.bu.edu/thurman/about /history, accessed March 2013.

When meditation teachers speak of the "power of now," it is *nunc stans* they are referring to. This expanded present is what we experience not only during meditation, but also during interludes in nature (as evoked by Wordsworth in his famous poem "Intimations of Immortality") while creating works of art, and in luminous moments of love. In *nunc stans*, the clock seems to stop, dropping us through the scrim of our everyday minds into great silence. Spaced-out as this may sound, we are actually more alert than usual during *nunc stans* moments, able to see more clearly and respond more effectively than when we are counting the minutes.

We need a bigger sense of time to help us accept what has not yet been revealed. We falsely imagine that what's in front of us is the end of the story; our objectifying minds tell us that what we see is what we get. But we do not know the long-term results of things, and this gives us a short-term take on time. This short-term perspective informs our actions, our giving, our caring. Maybe you give somebody a book and they don't react. So you think, *Well, that wasn't a big hit.* But years later, the person comes back and says something like, "You know, you gave me that book, and it didn't mean much to me at the time, but now my mother's very sick, and I picked up the book, and it was exactly what I needed." Sometimes, we're lucky and get some kind of feedback on our actions, but mostly, we're just planting seeds that ripple out in unknown directions that we may only hear about much later, if ever. An expanded sense of time teaches us that it is the act of planting the seed that really matters, not how and when—or even if—the flower grows.

Taking a long view brings an added sense of spaciousness, perspective, and wisdom. When things really hurt us, we may realize over time that they have opened us up in ways that enabled us to respond more wisely to similar situations later on. If we can live in this way, time is no longer the enemy.

CHAPTER 3

Victory over
the Secret Enemy

In working with the inner enemy, we overcame our subservi-
ence to the impulses of anger and hatred. As long as we continue to be mindful of the inner enemy and manage to resist its
demands, our body, speech, and mind will no longer be tools of
blind rage and compelling hatred. By understanding how blind
impulses had been controlling our actions, we began to find a
new inner freedom. Whereas previously we identified the voice
of anger as our own unquestioned voice and could not resist its
directives, once we saw that we have a plurality of voices in our
mind, we were able to draw on our common sense and reason,
and listen to the voice of wisdom that tells us we no longer
have to act on our impulses. Even after suffering harm, we can
choose a response that is calm, cool, and judicious, allowing
us to heal ourselves and prevent the person harming us from
causing more damage. Our actions are no longer mere reactions, so they tend to be much more effective.

But is this inner freedom that we now enjoy complete? Are
we sure that we can keep our cool at all times? If we are honest
with ourselves, we have to admit that there are depths in our
psyches that are beyond our mindful observation. Whatever is
inaccessible to our conscious awareness is, in a very real sense,

a secret we keep from ourselves. This is the secret enemy. We cannot be completely firm in our ability to control the inner enemy without uncovering the secret enemy and unlocking its secrets, bringing to consciousness what we were previously unaware of.

The secret enemy is an inner pattern that is deeply entwined with what Buddhist psychology calls the "self-habit," identified as the deepest root of desire, anger, and delusion. Built on the foundation of the identity habit, the secret enemy is the inner voice of self-preoccupation—"What about me? How am I doing? What am I getting out of it? What do I have? How do they see me? How will they serve me?" We listen raptly to this insistent, incessant ego voice and feel we cannot deny it, *because we think it is our only voice.* Yet this voice of our constant self-preoccupation is our deadliest enemy, insidiously powerful by pretending to be our true voice and seeming to be helpful and supportive, while actually leading us down the path to destruction. Hidden from our conscious mind by taking over our conscious mind, the secret enemy lives in the shadows, keeping itself secret from us by appearing to us as our very self.

SELF-PREOCCUPATION OR LOVING ONESELF?

Self-preoccupation is not the same thing as loving oneself. Self-preoccupation is the antithesis of what the Dalai Lama means when he says that he has never met anyone he would consider a stranger. When we are fixated on ourselves—which usually means being fixated on what we think is missing in ourselves or our lives—existence itself becomes our adversary. Instead of connecting with others, we hardly hear them above the din of our internal monologue: *What do they think about me? Do they like me? Do they like me more than they've ever liked anyone they've met before? Oh no, they hate me. I said something stupid. This is bad.* Locked inside this self-reflecting chamber, we cannot give, receive, or connect. Instead, our attention is focused on bolstering our own wobbly self-image and assuaging bleak feelings of emptiness.

When we genuinely connect with the world within us and around us, this burden is lifted. That is why it's so important to confront the many voices of the saboteurs, naysayers, and critics residing within our own minds if we hope not to make an enemy of others. Self-obsession breeds anger and contempt in others, inevitably leading to conflict.

The poet Wendell Berry, in defining the community as "the smallest unit of health," said that "to speak of the health of an isolated individual is a contradiction in terms."[9] Berry further defines a community as "a place and all its creatures." All the creatures that make up a community are interconnected. The healing of enmity and fear, then, is not something done at a remove from others, by oneself and for oneself. Instead, it calls for the recognition that we each exist as part of a greater fabric, a greater whole.

Interconnectedness means we are all going to make it together or not at all. The old idea of Us versus Them, which implies that it doesn't matter what happens to Them "over there"—wherever "there" is—is obsolete. We cannot afford to believe that everyday life isn't global or that what happens over there stays there. That is why, in these challenging times, there is such a resounding call for transformative social action that does not reify a rigid sense of the "other," is not based on hatred for anyone, and is looking for win-win solutions. The cost of having enemies is too high.

---

9   "Health Is Membership," in *The Art of the Commonplace: The Agrarian Essays of Wendell Berry* (Berkeley, CA: Counterpoint Press), p. 146.

It doesn't take a particularly spiritual view to see this. Environmental understanding confirms that we are all connected. Epidemiology confronts us with that same certain truth of interdependence, as borders are proven again and again to be conceptual constructs, and economics reminds us of it as well—that somehow what happens in Greece has an effect on my life in a small town in Massachusetts.

When we're mindful, life shows us how connected, in fact, we really are. It is apparent through all of life's twists and turns—when we face difficulties, when we confront the fragility of circumstances, when we share our own happiness with others, when we are willing to meet a stranger in a new way.

The secret enemy stands firmly planted upon our ingrained self-habit, our fixed-identity habit. But what exactly is this fixed-identity habit? It's that feeling we have that we are always the same person, a fixed subjectivity, and that our identity stays the same in all circumstances throughout our life. When you see a picture of yourself in your youth—as a teenager, say— you feel as if you are still the same person as your younger self, even though a moment's reflection tells you that not a single cell in your body is the same. The experience of unchanging persistence is what we call the identity habit or, at the deepest unconscious level, the "identity instinct."

The sense of always being the same self that constitutes the identity instinct or habit gives me the impression that at any given time, I am perceiving my "real self." The absolute conviction that *I am here* becomes the seemingly concrete basis of my continual preoccupation with myself—my self-centeredness, my selfishness, my possessiveness. And it is this preoccupation with myself that keeps me in a constant state of frustration and dissatisfaction, feeling that I am never loved enough, never have enough, never *am* enough.

But as we can easily see, when I investigate this habitual sense of self, turning my self-centeredness back on itself, I'm unable to find anything stable and enduring that can be pinpointed as *the real me*. I can find parts of my body and its processes. I can find fleeting moments of sensations, thoughts, and ideas. I can find words and images that rise and fall—and feelings and emotions entangled with those sensations, words, and images. I can even become aware of awareness itself, keeping and losing track of it all. But nowhere do I find my imagined concrete, fixed, and independent self.

The deeper we dig, the more we recognize that our sense of self-perception is a delusion, an error. As we focus on the recognition that our sense of self-perception is a delusion, our continuous self-preoccupation begins to feel hollow, and its compelling flow becomes less overwhelming. Our self-sense begins to sputter—we may even feel as if we're going crazy—and in the gaps we forget for an instant who it is we're trying to be and find ourselves lost in our surroundings. Momentarily freed of our rigid sense of self, we are startled to find ourselves connecting with something other than ourselves, released from the squirrel cage of, as George Harrison of the Beatles put it, "I, me, me, mine."

As a structure of the unconscious, the secret enemy has the force of instinct, while at a more conscious level, it operates as habit. It manifests by shutting us away from reality and other people, so that we focus only on our own self-condition. Wound tight within, the secret enemy reinforces the illusion that there is a solid structure at its core. But it is like a knot in a shoelace that looks so firm until we pull apart the tips of the lace and realize there is no firm core. One of the Buddha's great achievements was to discover the knotted structure of the fixed self-sense and untangle it, to see that its solidity is merely an illusion. And once we experience the illusoriness of the seemingly solid self, we are released from its thrall. No longer dominated by the unconscious fixation on self and the conscious habit of self-preoccupation, we are able to experience and enjoy real inner freedom.

Working with the Secret Enemy

It is common animal and human nature to think we have a stable core identity. The self-habit is the anchor of our sense of existence and the backstop of our awareness in the world. We persist in thinking that this *I* is the real me, the absolute, independent, self-sufficient, intrinsically undeniable self. And we tend to assume that if we analytically dissected all our conscious experience, sense impressions, thoughts and emotions, highs and lows, we would end up colliding with this absolute self. So when we hear the word *selfless*, we react on two levels. At first, we might think of Florence Nightingale or Gandhi or military heroes—people who sacrifice themselves for the sake of others. Selfless in this sense means being capable of setting aside the hard core of self for a higher calling. On a deeper level, however, *selfless* as a philosophical and psychological negation technically denies the existence of the absolute self we think is the anchor of our existence, telling us simply that it is a misperception, an illusion. Initially, when we understand selflessness in this way, our reaction is likely to be fear, even terror, or irritation, even dismay. Selflessness challenges our unexamined way of experiencing ourselves, and so the world.

This mistaken sense of a fixed, independent self—the secret enemy's ground of the identity-habit—supports its partner, unrelenting self-obsession and self-preoccupation. Digging around in the unconscious at the level of instinct can be overwhelming, so we need powerful help in order not to run away at the first sign of fear. Happily, in our struggle with the secret enemy and its basic support, we can turn to an eminent 11th-century Buddhist teacher and poet, master Dharmarakshita. He left us a vivid record of his own battle with the secret enemy in his masterwork in Tibetan, *Lojong Tsoncha Khorlo,* which translates as *The Blade Wheel of Mind Reform.*

Dharmarakshita identified four basic steps to victory over

the secret enemy. (1) The first challenge is finding the secret enemy, the constant self-preoccupation that is based on the self-identity complex as both instinct and habit. (2) Once we find it, we need to observe it and, with penetrating focus, mindfully experience how it works within us, at both the level of habit and the level unconscious instinct. (3) Becoming conscious of the secret enemy does not immediately rid us of its ill effects, however. It takes time to flush it out and erode it—to correct our misperception with wisdom, and cultivate self-preoccupation's antidote, other-preoccupation. (4) And finally, we have to deepen our critical understanding of the secret enemy by means of meditative concentration, to go deep enough to uproot the underlying instinctual pattern, reach the welling bliss of inner freedom, and seal our release from the secret enemy.

The four-step path to victory over the secret enemy is a gradual process, requiring critical wisdom and meditative concentration, creative perseverance in mental and social action, and, ultimately, the courageous ability to tolerate freedom and bliss. It requires true heroism.

This is where *The Blade Wheel of Mind Reform* comes in. What does this title mean? The blade wheel is a sharp weapon, a small circle of blades sometimes called a throwing star. It is a symbol of the critical wisdom with which we terminate the secret enemy. Dharmarakshita teaches us that the secret enemy is like a devil, a relentless foe that has captured us and imprisoned us in our sleepwalking life. This unawakened life of self-absorption admits no real connection to other people or the world around us; it allows no real openness to human warmth and love. It is a kind of living death. Dharmarakshita provides us with a wheel weapon of teaching to conquer this devil-enemy—a life-saving weapon against egotism and selfishness.

Mind reform is mental transformation through the steps to awaken from the sleep of narcissism. It is not a matter of imparting new information or skills to the same old mind, but rather a systematic work of expanding and opening the mind itself, freeing it from debilitating old confusions and fears, and focusing it on its own natural openness and responsiveness. This expanded mind must be cultivated, and Dharmarakshita offers us a method to do so.

After my original teacher, the Venerable Geshe Wangyal, had spent a couple of years correcting me and exposing my self-preoccupation and self-addiction, he presented the blade-wheel teaching to me as the bottom line of the liberating teaching of the Buddha, usually called the "Dharma." Just as the Ninjas used the weapons we call throwing stars to cut up their enemies, the blade wheel bears down on our secret enemy, seriously damaging narcissism, vanity, and persistent self-concern. The blade wheel is a very fierce image for mental transformation, a fiercer form of Manjushri's surgical blade of critical wisdom. The wisdom of ultimate reality will not indulge any of our self-habit-based selfish concerns; it will slice them to ribbons. We don't have to wonder if this process will work. Our own determined intelligence and emotional honesty have the power to overwhelm our self-identity habit and break us out of the iron cage of self-preoccupation.

This victory over the ingrained selfish instinct that imprisons us is truly apocalyptic, in the sense of being immediate in its revelatory power. It doesn't let us sit around and wait for some future life in which we will attain enlightenment. It aims to destroy the secret enemy now.

In cutting down the secret enemy it is important to have a model of enlightenment. We awaken to blissful, free, intuitive wisdom in this lifetime, so it should be someone—a teacher or therapist or spiritual guide, perhaps—who embodies these qualities. You could choose Dharmarakshita as your model, or Shantideva, whom we met in Chapter 2, or the Dalai Lama or Jesus or Buddha—or any other mentor whose quality of being inspires you.

Finding the Secret Enemy

As you ferret out the secret enemy and deal with it, you will want to carry around the vision of your enlightened teacher, because at the beginning of this process, your point of reference is your habitual vision of the world, which is likely to be more garbage heap than heaven or the pure land paradises of the buddhas. While you are unawakened, your focus will be on yourself, with thoughts like *What can I get? Where do I fit in? Are they doing what I want? Is it good enough? Are they meeting my needs?* These attitudes are the last sputterings of the demon of self-concern, the bars on your prison walls, the ring in your nose by which the secret enemy is leading you around. At this point, you identify totally with your enemy and captor, self-addiction.

The true mentor—the real spiritual guide—is the wisdom of ultimate reality present at the deepest level of the life force within your heart. It manifests as the person who challenges you to find this demon, but it sparks your own intuitive wisdom to locate the enemy within and eliminate it. It is not the mentor who liberates you; it is your own understanding that attacks the enemy you falsely believe is preventing you from releasing your liberating understanding.

As we find the secret enemy, we come to see how our self-preoccupation kills our relationships, which are the source of our life energy. Egotism mistakenly thinks it can draw energy from the imagined absolute self, but how can it draw energy from something that does not exist? The absolute self is only a mental construct, a fantasy, a mirror in a hall of mirrors that seems to reflect something that is not there.

Mind reform involves figuring out how to take all the negative things that happen to us—loss, pain, failure, the hostility of others—and make something positive out of them. The first step is to take responsibility for everything bad that happens to us and not to assign blame to our outer enemies. Working to liberate ourselves from the secret enemy requires us to invest all our energy in our own internal evolution rather than in struggling against people and events in our environment. *The Blade Wheel* goes to great lengths to cite misfortune after misfortune that befall us, and then shows us how to accept it as the result of our own previous negative action, seeing it like a boomerang that we threw in our previous life or lives, which circled back to hit us. Thus, when I lose my homeland, it is because I took others' lands away from them in the past. When my house burns down, it is because I burned out others long back. When I lose my relationships, it is because I broke up others' relationships in the past. And on and on. We basically blame the victim—ourselves only in a deep evolutionary sense—in order to take responsibility for everything and empower ourselves, never more to be helpless as a victim! And then we add to that new empowerment our discovery of the secret enemy as the one who dominated us in our evolutionary past and caused us to selfishly do all these things to others, which we are now returning to us. This then strengthens our resolve to recognize the secret enemy and stand up to it, in order not to follow its dictates and do anything negative toward anyone ever again.

Observing the Secret Enemy

This important step in achieving victory over the secret enemy requires us to radically change our narrative about the past, move away from being the helpless victim, and empower ourselves to be the active agent of our own life and evolutionary destiny. Instead of continuing to complain about my environment, for example, I acknowledge that I have always viewed whatever is going on around me as flawed, owing to my own imperfect perception. Now, instead of looking at the world and seeing only the evils and ugliness and people harming one another, I turn my back on my misplaced certainty and purify my perception.

Consider, for example, environmental activists. They are the heroes of the present planetary crisis, but their effectiveness can be severely hampered if they get caught in the misperception that the situation is hopeless, that the polluters will never reform, and that their protests will fall on deaf ears and ultimately fail to halt the destruction. To be effective, they must turn their attention within and find the root of their despair, and then approach each situation without prejudging the outcome, inspiring themselves and others with hope.

One practice we could do to empower our vision for a better world is a "perfection of perception" visualization, in which we systematically transform our ordinary environment into the perfect world of the mandala, the mind-protecting perfect space for cultivating confidence and creativity. In visualizing our everyday life as such a mandala, we imagine that we are in a magic universe where everything is made of pure jewel-like energy, where the mountains and clouds are all exquisite, where everything is the reality of bliss and freedom, and there is no dirt, no garbage, no pollution—nothing negative.

This kind of visualization practice moves you onto a subtle plane where you abandon your habitual investment in the world of ordinariness and turn your critical attention upon yourself. When the outside world looks bad or your mentor seems flawed, you can invert those perceptions and take them as your own failure of perception. Corrupt politicians, food shortages, wars, terrorism—we contemplate even these as projections of our own imperfections. Observing the enemy in this way involves taking responsibility for creating the world as an impure, imperfect place. To assist us in turning our perception around, we can repeat the following thought.

All the imperfections I perceive have to do with my faulty vision. Every time I have a negative perception of something, I will challenge it radically and overcome my habitual perception of ordinariness. This is the purification of perception.

Reenvisioning the world as the best of all possible worlds is a very radical practice. It calls for an internal revolution, a total change of mind. Using your critical faculty, you see clearly that everything is free of any fixed, substantial core, that everything is relative. You realize that relative reality is fluid, not fixed, that it is multifaceted, ambiguous, and cognitively dissonant, simultaneously ordinary and extraordinary. You decide that you can change yourself, and others can change themselves, so everything is possible. You free yourself from despair and release your creativity in every situation.

We practice purifying our perception in order to stop blaming everybody else, to stop seeing all the faults in the world as caused by others, and instead take those faults upon ourselves. This empowers us to do something about ourselves and take responsibility for our future. If we see that bad things happen to us as the result of our own past negative actions and perceptions, we can turn everything around. By this radical flip, we see everything as the best of all possible worlds. As aspiring bodhisattvas, awakening heroes, we vow to make this world the best of all possible worlds for all beings.

The only way we can really change a situation is to completely master our own reaction to it. Self-control gives us power. In taking responsibility when bad things happen to us and embracing these problems as our own construction, we stop demonizing others. When someone harms us, we don't get mad or bewail our fate. We think: *This is happening in order to purify me of my previous negative actions. The buddhas and deities and angels are teaching me in this way. It's so kind of them.*

At first, everything in us rebels against this practice. *Isn't this masochistic?* we might think. But far from masochistic, taking responsibility in this way is a loving thing to do for ourselves. Like the extraction of a rotten tooth, it may be painful in the short run, but it removes the potential for far more misery in the long run.

Shantideva said, "If you don't like to step on thorns and sharp rocks as you walk around the planet, you have two choices. You can either pave the whole earth with shoe leather, or you can make yourself a pair of sandals." Mind-reform is making sandals for our souls.

EMPATHY

Science is teaching us intriguing things about how empathy, our ability to identify with others' feelings, develops. The discovery in the 1990s of a class of cells in the brain called mirror neurons suggests a new understanding of how we learn to get along with one another. Current understanding considers mirror neurons the brain's hardware for harmonizing individuals with their environment. The sole purpose of these neurons seems to be to mirror in our brains the actions we observe in others, to facilitate feeling what they feel. "Mirror neurons allow us to grasp the minds of others not through conceptual reasoning but through direct simulation. By feeling, not by thinking,"[10] explains Giacomo Rizzolatti, the scientist who led the team that made this discovery.

A newborn baby, barely able to see, can imitate the facial expressions of adults within one hour of delivery. From the doting look in its mother's eyes, the baby draws its earliest, wordless lessons about connection, care, and love—and learns, too, how being ignored makes those good feelings disappear.

It is because of mirror neurons that we yawn when we see someone else yawn, flinch when somebody else is struck, and laugh when the people around us break out

10   Quoted in Sandra Blakeslee, "Cells That Read Minds," *The New York Times,* January 10, 2006, www.nytimes.com.

in giggles. (Indeed, people who test high for "contagious yawning" are found to be more empathic.) Mirror neurons are considered to be the reason why emotions—both negative and positive—can sometimes be as contagious as the flu. Imagine: the brain itself might well be built to allow us to bridge the Us-versus-Them divide and experience others as if from inside their own skin.

Researcher Barbara Fredrickson takes this notion a step further in offering a new concept of how we connect with one another, based on what she calls "micro-moments of positivity resonance."[11] Love, she says, consists of these micro-moments shared not just with our nearest and dearest but with anyone we make a connection with in the ordinary course of our day—a work colleague, a waiter at the coffee shop, even a stranger. The course of action she has studied in her research is lovingkindness meditation. Barbara comments, "Love, from your body's perspective, is a biological wave of good feeling and mutual care that rolls through two or more brains and bodies at once. Your body needs these micro-moments of positivity resonance just like it needs good food and physical activity. . . . The more of these micro-moments you each have, the more each of you grows happier, healthier, and wiser."[12]

These "blasts" of positive emotion flowing between us and others "build the very bonds that have kept [us] alive," Fredrickson says.[13]

The science of positivity resonance involves mirror neurons, the hormone oxytocin, and a condition called vagal tone. Oxytocin makes us feel more trusting and open to

11   Barbara Fredrickson, Love 2.0: How Our Supreme Emotion Affects Everything We Feel, Think, Do, and Become (New York: Hudson Street Press, 2013), p. 35.

12   Barbara Fredrickson, "The Big Idea: Barbara Fredrickson on Love," The Daily Beast, February 14, 2013, http://www.thedailybeast.com/articles/2013/02/14/the-big-idea-barbara-fredrickson-on-love-2-0.html.

13   Barbara Fredrickson, Love 2.0: How Our Supreme Emotion Affects Everything We Feel, Think, Do, and Become (New York: Hudson Street Press, 2013), p. 29.

connection, and it is the hormone of bonding and attachment that spikes during micro-moments of love. Vagal tone relates to activity of the vagus nerve, which connects the brain to the heart and other organs, and affects a person's potential for love. As Fredrickson explains, "your vagus nerve stimulates tiny facial muscles that better enable you to make eye contact and synchronize your facial expressions with another person. It even adjusts the minuscule muscles of your middle ear so you can better track the other person's voice against any background noise."[14]

The brain, nervous systems, and hormones all seem to be primed for resonance. Empathy, even love, may be much closer at hand than we realize.

In the process of mind reform, it is very important to consider with whom we associate. The reality of interconnectedness is that we are highly influenced by the people we hang out with. If we associate with enlightened people who have more insight, kindness, and wisdom than we do, those qualities will rub off on us. If we keep company with people who are negative, deluded, or self-destructive, we will become like them. Above all, it is important not to hang out with the secret enemy, our self-preoccupation habit. Self-preoccupation is the worst friend to adopt and the best one to drop. The very best way to drop the self-preoccupation habit, to erode it gradually, is to replace it with other-preoccupation. Instead of always focusing on what we are getting out of whatever, we focus on what others are getting out of it. We think about them and that stream of altruistic thoughts crowds out the previously habitual stream of self-preoccupied thoughts. The transformation that gradually ensues from carefully doing this becomes the engine of mind-reform. This daily practice,

---

14 Ibid., p. 54.

a meditation-in-action practice, is called "the exchange of self and other," and it is the heart practice of both Shantideva and Dharmarakshita.

Mind reform is a powerful method for managing the interpersonal relationships that make up everyday life. It is one thing to go and meditate alone in a cave and another to develop a mind practice that works on interpersonal relations. We can develop compassion only through interacting with one another—and, realistically, we are always interacting with others. The meditation known as give-and-take practice can help us develop awareness of how we behave in our daily social interactions.

GIVE-AND-TAKE PRACTICE

The meditation of give and take is a way to begin to neutralize the hostility and fear of our enemies. We imagine that we give away our happiness to others and take their suffering upon ourselves. We relieve our enemies of their hostility by adopting their perspective and feeling the tension and stress they feel in being angry with us and wanting to harm us. We accept the enemy's anger and let it overwhelm our own egotistical self, which wants to harm the enemy in return for the harm it thinks the enemy is directing at us. In this way, we redirect the enemy's aggression into helping us conquer our own habitual negative feelings and responses.

In give-and-take meditation, we imaginatively take on the pain and suffering of others, including our enemies, with our inhalations, as if we were inhaling clouds of smoke. Then we let the pain and suffering dissolve into the openness of our heart, which has broken free of the identity habit. And finally, with our exhalation we give out the light of bliss that wells up from the depths of the liberated heart and flows out to others. (See Appendix, page 166, for more detailed instructions on the practice of give and take.)

Give and take is a liberating meditation. In imagining that we let the enemy have the victory over our ego-self, we disidentify with the self-cherishing, self-preoccupied, what-about-me mind and replace it with the shining, altruistic mind focused on benefiting everyone. Instead of suffering over harm that comes our way, we can hold this thought:

How happy I am that this has happened. Every ounce of pain it gives me is welcome, because it enables me to atone for the negative things I have done to others, for the harm I have caused others in the past. In the future I will not heedlessly misuse or abuse others. I will abandon harmful ways.

Give-and-take meditation is an empowering way to handle suffering and turn it to our benefit. When, for example, we come down with a sickness that seems to have come out of the blue, if we can accept that the illness is coming to us from our previously reckless, careless, or insensitive actions, we can use it as a constructive practice. Some teachings hold that even natural disasters come from having broken various vows in previous lives: religious vows, secular vows, all sorts of vows. You may find this hard to accept, but think about it. At the very least, consider how many natural disasters today are the result of humans having broken a collective vow to honor our responsibility as custodians of the earth. So when tornadoes strike, don't shake your fist at God or Nature, but turn your distress into a personal vow: *In the future I shall abandon all negative actions.*

Viewing natural disasters as the consequence of our own harmful actions does not mean we should walk away from people who are suffering from such disasters, however. We must make every effort to help them. The meditation of give and take is simply a way for us to turn whatever disasters we experience into precious opportunities for inner transformation.

LOOKING FOR THE GOOD

Kindness is a potent tool for transformation, since it requires us to step outside our conditioned response patterns. Ordinarily, we're so preoccupied with ourselves and defended against the Other—especially in these terrorist, orange-alert times—that we feel continually threatened and anxious. We forget how connected to one another we are, and this perceived division feeds our antipathy and feelings of alienation. This limited perspective prompts us to respond in ways that are less creative, reducing the possibilities for happiness.

When I was first learning lovingkindness meditation in Burma, one of the preliminary exercises was to look for the good in someone, even in someone you didn't like. On hearing those instructions, my first thought was, *That's silly! I'm not going to do that. That's what stupid people do—they go around looking for the good in people. And I don't even like people who are like that!*

Nonetheless, I followed my teacher's instructions and had an eye-opening experience as a result. I thought of someone whose behavior I generally found irritating and obnoxious. Then I had a memory of seeing him do something beautiful for a mutual friend. Immediately I thought, *I don't want to look at that! It will just complicate things!* It was a lot easier to keep going over his faults, to keep him the box marked "enemy" and "this one I don't like."

Our default position seems to be the belief that people are fixed entities rather than ever-changing beings with a whole range of possible behaviors. Seeing others in all their complexity requires emotional intelligence; it represents a major step in psychological development. Our first lesson in emotional complexity comes when we are children. At first we see our parents as all good and then later as all bad. As we mature, ideally, we arrive at an understanding that

the truth lies somewhere in the middle: our parents are neither all good nor all bad but a mixture of both. Unless we
can accept this inherent ambiguity, we will miss the complexity of other people, as well as the ability to be flexible
in our attitudes toward them. Even when we can't seem
to find something good about someone, we can remind
ourselves of what we have in common. Every human being
is vulnerable to change, loss, and insecurity. And every
human being wants to be happy, regardless of how misguided their efforts might seem to be.

In the Koran, God tells humanity, "We made you . . .
into nations and tribes that ye might know one another."[15]
This affirmation of the oneness of humanity, despite the
distinctions of nation and tribe, expresses the understanding that such distinctions should lead to a better understanding of each other, not enmity. Just as we could not
practice patience without annoyance or compassion without enemies, we could not do away with duality, Us versus
Them, without significant differences to overcome.

A VOW OF ALTRUISM

By now you may be convinced that stubborn self-seeking is
the secret enemy. When we can't put a stop to our anger at
others, when everything we do makes us dissatisfied and frus-
trates others, the culprit is our ancient habit of self-seeking and
our persistent self-preoccupation. When we constantly miss
our goals, it is the blade wheel of our negative karma boomer-
anging against us from the past, driven by our instinctual and
habitual immersion in narrow selfishness.

What we need to do now is to be altruistic without fail.
Motivation is the key. We need to constantly examine and
reform our motivation. If we do great things but they never

---

15 Yusuf Ali translation, 49:13.

seem to succeed, perhaps our motivation was narrowly selfish. If we seek fame and profit only for ourselves, the greatest deed will go sour. We will feel unsatisfied and want more, and others will sense the lack of heart in our efforts and lose interest. But when we give up focusing on ourselves, even without achieving great deeds, we will feel good.

From now on, we can make a vow to create the spirit of enlightenment, the altruistic attitude of the bodhisattva. Here is an exercise to help cultivate this attitude, overcoming the obsession with I, me, me, mine:

> Remember a time when you were content with what you had, when you saw the glass as half full. You were not focused on your narrow selfish vision of *What do I have? How much is mine?* You were not thinking about "I, me, me, mine." So when an ant crawled across your arm, instead of swatting it, you took the time to put it somewhere safe, to save its life.
>
> Remember a time when you listened attentively to something new a friend said. In fact, because your attention was turned outward toward the other person, you were temporarily unconcerned with yourself.
>
> Now make this vow: May everything I do be only altruistic. May I always attend to the world. May I be concerned about whether others are happy. May I be altruistic in little ways. May I be other-preoccupied instead of self-preoccupied.

This is the altruistic turnaround. It is a crucial step in defeating the secret enemy. When we misunderstand altruism, we think that if we are other-preoccupied, we will destroy ourselves and suffer more. But the irony is, when we take on others' discomforts, we become happier and stronger, unbothered by whatever misery we encounter.

The paradoxes of life are always like this. When we are

stingy we always feel poor, because we can never have enough. Even if we have billions, if we are focused only on how much more we can get and beating out our rivals to get it, we still feel dissatisfied. We lose a few million and feel deep agony, in spite of our remaining billions, whereas someone with next to nothing can be happy with whatever little they have, if they are preoccupied with someone else's well-being. True wealth is contentment, and happiness is forgetting to worry how you are and how much you have.

Taking a Long View

Most people in the West remain totally preoccupied with the goals of this life because we don't believe there is another life. We think this life is all we have, so we're conditioned to getting whatever we can, the sooner the better. Although it is possible for people with this attitude to be altruistic and help others, their primary motivation remains acquiring benefits in this life.

We can, however, go beyond this thinking and realize that this very moment is infinite. Within the present moment are the qualities of our past and future lives. It is like Nietzsche's concept of "eternal recurrence": everything we do, he said, we should be willing to redo for eternity. Everything we do reverberates for eternity, so our ultimate concern should be the quality of how we live now. When we presume that we will be nothing after death, not consciously present in the future, then we lose touch with the infinity of this moment. If we think this moment is all there is, we have no power to overcome our automatic reactions to things, no power to rise above our greed and anger. We don't think our behavior has long-term consequences: *So what if I blow my cool today? I'll be better tomorrow, and I'll only feel bad from now until then.* How different our response would be if we truly realized that the way we behave today is infinite in its consequences. It is in controlling the mind that we gain a true sense of the infinity of the moment, the realization that freedom is right here now.

When the mind remains uncontrolled, it is because we are preoccupied with the goals of this life. Our arrogance and selfish ambition throw us off balance. So we need to work on detachment to overcome our enemy of self-preoccupation, our habitual focus on I, me, me, mine. The less greedy we are, the less needy we are. The more content we become, the less easily fooled we are by others. Gullibility is based upon selfish ambition.

When it seems as if nothing ever turns out right, then everything we do will be unsatisfying, no matter how worthwhile it is. We can go on a pilgrimage to holy places, but then we get carsick on the winding roads, the car breaks down, we squabble nonstop with our traveling companions, and there is no food to eat. No matter how uplifting the trip, we fail to appreciate it, thinking that we should go faster or slower, or be somewhere else; that there should be more people or fewer people; that the weather should be better. When we are not content with our present situation, it is because we were ungrateful in the past, either this life or a previous. We projected our own self-seeking onto others' motives and so could not trust or accept their kindness.

When we grasp that every action has immense consequences, we become super-aware of what we do. "Super-aware" means knowing the subtle details of our actions. The tiniest selfish motivation or self-centered thought or slight misstep can have a huge negative effect. That's where knowledge of ultimate reality comes in. The idea that the ultimate reality, or the absolute—nirvana or heaven—is a place to which we can float away is based on the delusion of being an absolute, fixed, essential self separate from the world. Unable to find nirvana within ourselves, we project it outward into some imagined space beyond space. But just as there is no separate self within us, there is no nirvana or heaven out there somewhere. Nirvana/heaven is here and now—this world as experienced by an altruistic being, a truly other-preoccupied, infinitely expanded being. Enlightenment isn't supernatural: it is simply super-awareness of the minute details of life and their infinite consequences.

Flushing Out the Secret Enemy

Now we bear down on the life-changing, transformative insight that opens the door to true happiness: the awareness that the source of all our troubles, directly or indirectly, is the secret enemy, our self-addiction. How amazing it is to realize that my secret enemy is my own self-habit, my own doomed effort to be "the real me." This is the thief who repeatedly attacked and robbed me; what a relief to have identified him. Now I can try to get my treasure back.

At this point we feel triumphant and delighted: *Now I know the real enemy. I see that there isn't some evil person out there after me.* This is the key. When your self-preoccupied mind says, "This is a really good idea. You'll get something great out of it. Go grab it," it is fooling you, because you think it is your own irresistible impulse. You are helpless in the face of its dictates, because it presents itself as your own thought. But when you recognize that demon, when you see clearly that it is the mental habit itself that is the enemy, then you are free.

Now that you have identified the secret enemy, you are never going to doubt again. Tired of being the target of the blade wheel of negative karma as it slices you to ribbons again and again, you can finally grab the blade wheel of selfless wisdom and cut down your self-fixation. "Let it come," you say. "Hit me with all my negative habits—fear, anger, selfish desire. Because now I know who the real enemy is. When the blade wheel of negative evolution comes at me, I can let it go right through the real, living me to hit its target, my devil of self-preoccupation, tangled around the devil of self-habit." The super-formula that completes your freedom is altruism: love and compassion, pure other-concern. Altruism is a positive addiction—addiction to the happiness and freedom of other beings.

There are four medicinal forces that, taken together, are said to be the fangs, the dog teeth that mash up the secret enemy of self-addiction: confession, repentance, the resolve to be positive, and the intuitive awareness of freedom. These medicinal forces are not just some gimmick; they offer a remedy that works. First, we must genuinely confess to or acknowledge the negative things we have done. Really face them. Next, we must be genuinely repentant that we have done them. Then, we must form a genuine resolve not to do them again. Finally, we must see that there was no good reason to have done them and there is no excuse to repeat them. This is where we break the chain. Repentance alone is not enough. Ultimately, we have to see through our wrongdoing. When we truly see that there is nothing concrete or binding about our transgressions, we can break free from them and never have to do such things again. There are an infinite number of transgressions and an infinite amount of bad consequences, so infinite freedom is the final goal.

Freedom from self-addiction is real victory. The turnaround is that we face ourselves, see through ourselves, and then ignore ourselves and become preoccupied with others. We develop an awareness that is other-oriented. This is true enlightenment practice and really profound. Other-preoccupation does not come in a blinding flash. It comes upon us gently, quietly, gradually, as our hard-edged self-conviction slowly melts in the warmth of connection to others and the natural world.

FROM ME TO WE

The philosopher Martin Buber defined two kinds of human relationships, which he termed *I-Thou* and *I-It*. In I-Thou relationships, we come to the relationship without preconditions, reaching out to each other as individuals and forming a bond. In I-It relationships, on the other hand, we treat one another as objects, as functionaries, as a means to our own ends. When you speak to the clerk in the checkout line at the supermarket, are you talking to a person or to a cash register? Would you even remember the name on her name tag, never mind anything she had to say? When we are self-preoccupied, we dehumanize the people we encounter, sometimes with painful consequences. Learning to pay attention to the other person can reverse the effect. As the psychologist Daniel Goleman, who popularized the concept of emotional intelligence, has said, "Empathy is the prime inhibitor of human cruelty."[16]

I experienced a poignant example of this recently when a friend and I went out to dinner. My friend is a recovering alcoholic who prizes her sobriety. As we were walking down the street, we were approached by a homeless man asking for money. Had I been alone, I regret to admit that I might have handed the man a bit of change and then hurried on without even looking him in the eye. But my friend, who has a great deal of empathy for the suffering of addiction, had quite a different response. Not wanting to possibly enable a substance abuser, she told him, "Instead of money, I'd like to invite you to the deli so you can get whatever you want to eat." The man could not have been more elated. Having so little choice in his life, he savored the novelty of being treated with respect, as an individual with his own needs and desires. I learned a lot from watching this exchange.

As my friend's actions showed, empathy and compassion do not necessarily mean that we automatically give people whatever they want, any more than lovingkindness means being meek and always saying yes. (Sometimes the

16 Daniel Goleman, *Social Intelligence: The New Science of Human Relationships* (New York: Bantam, 2006) p. 117.

loving response is no.) It simply means that we are relating to the other as a person and not as a symbol, a concept, a label, or an adversary. Relating in this way allows appropriate responses to arise from wisdom. The thread of connection is always there if we remember to notice it.

We are continually being chased by the vicious demon of self-habit—this does not stop just because we become aware of the problem. So we must invoke the compassionate force of our own liberated intelligence to turn our ego-addiction against itself. We invoke Manjushri, the embodiment of the transcendent wisdom of selflessness, in his fiercest form, Yamantaka, Death-Exterminator, whom we met briefly in Chapter 1. Yamantaka destroys our deadly habit of self-obsession. When we see through the delusion of a solid self, we touch the transparency of all things, and our intrinsic self-centeredness opens up to natural blissfulness. The more we realize that, the more blissful we become.

We need wisdom's powerful help to free ourselves from our secret enemy, since our self-obsession is our jailer. Imprisoned in our habitual identity and defending it against the world, we are unable to experience the new and the fresh. But the jailer is as much imprisoned as the prisoner, chained to his post outside the cell to make sure the prisoner stays inside. So the self-habit is torture all the way around. It is like the family dog, growling and scratching and resisting terribly until the porcupine quill is finally extricated from its jaw—at which point it leaps up, overjoyed, smothering you with kisses at having been freed from pain.

When we call on wisdom to liberate the enemy—to get rid of the jailer and break us out of prison—we also liberate the prison keeper. Liberating the ego from a distorted and obsessively rigid role frees it to become truly relational and truly loving. Wisdom does not destroy the self, because there is no independent self to destroy. It is the illusion of a fixed, rigid self that wisdom destroys.

The Buddha did not teach selflessness in a dogmatic manner. He sometimes spoke of someone who "has the self under control," or "frees the self from delusion." Now and then he did say, "There is no self," just to shock people out of their illusions, because he knew that when we hear *self,* we think first of the illusory self. But over the millennia, as the Buddha's teachings were reported out of context, phrases like *There is no self* and *I don't exist* were erroneously said to be evidence of Buddhist nihilism. The Buddha was well aware that he was sitting there talking, and that people saw and heard him talking, and that it would be madness for him to say, "I don't exist." What he meant was, "I don't exist the way I thought I existed." Similarly, when he said, "There is no table," he meant that the table doesn't exist as something with its own intrinsic, fixed essence. But clearly the table is something I can slap my hand against. So let's not imagine that getting rid of the secret enemy of self-preoccupation means we are supposed to destroy ourselves.

The self that *does* exist and cannot ultimately be destroyed is the relative self. Habitually under the cruel domination of the false notion of an absolute self, the relative self suffers, never able to match up to our notion of the absolute self. Not rigid or fixed, the relative self is flexible, vulnerable, ever-changing. This relative self is not a thing, a separate entity, but a process that includes a body, an embodied mind, sometimes called a "coarse mind," and a soul,[17] or "subtle mind." The relative self is the living self—the conventional self who makes the children breakfast, goes to work, and kisses its loved ones at night. When we get rid of the delusory overlay on the relative self, then at last it becomes a buddha-self, perfect even within its imperfections.

---

17 The word "soul" is used by Western translators of Buddhist texts to translate Sanskrit *atma* (Pali, *atta*), and, since they tend to want to escape the Christian idea of "immortal soul" that can go on to heaven or hell, they argue that Buddha discovered that there was no such thing as "soul." Sometimes Buddha did say there is no soul, in the same passages where he says there is no eye, no ear, no nose, etc., always meaning "no absolute soul, eye, ear, etc." So, since we do have relative eyes, ears, etc., we can certainly also have a relative soul, a selfless soul, if you will, using the familiar term to describe the ever-changing mental continuum, super-subtle drop, or spiritual gene, which is what we are as we move from life to life.

So selflessness does not mean that the relative self is destroyed. We do not even trample the ego or toss it away. The ego is just the pronoun *I*. We strengthen it to make it resilient as an instrument to relate to the workaday world. Liberating yourself from trying to be a fixed, absolute self allows you to become the relative self.

Clear awareness about the relative self, the conventional self, is one of the keys to accomplishing liberation. The self is only the self by virtue of being verbally as well as mentally designated as the self. The pronouns *I* and *you* create the "I" and "you."

When you get rid of your self-involvement and release yourself to become absorbed in your work, for example—wow, no self! (Psychologists use the term *flow* for this state of being fully immersed in an activity without conscious awareness of self, first observed by researcher Mihaly Csikszentmihalyi. So the risking of self, the forgetting of self, the release of self-concern, is not such a far-out concept. Ordinary life requires it of us in order to get things done. An athlete who is "in the zone" has, for the moment, gotten rid of the secret enemy of self-obsession. For us, the practice is learning to live in the zone, even outside the sports arena.

THE TYRANNY OF SEPARATION

We can get lost in the Us-versus-Them thinking that undergirds enemy-making when we fall into the narcissistic assumption that we are the center of the universe. This is the not-so-subtle tyranny of self-preoccupation and sense of entitlement.

When Hurricane Irene swept up the East Coast in 2011, washing away whole communities and stranding tens of thousands without power or heat, because New York City was largely spared, many people there dismissed the severity of the storm as "media hype." But if you lived in upstate New York or a Vermont town submerged under six feet of water, there wasn't a whole lot of hype to the devastating effect on your life. If we have any hope of feeling empathy for others, we have to be able to enlarge our perspective when we view the world.

In a similar way, the restorative-justice movement contends that when offenders are confronted with the wider consequence of their actions, instead of holding on to likely justifications—"No one will be hurt." "They can afford the loss."—many experience a shift in their defensive, adversarial thinking. For example, a thief might be told that because he had stolen from a certain gas station, the owner was downsizing to try to recoup his loss and his increased insurance premiums. The owner had to lay off one of his employees, who was struggling to support his sister. Without his help, she couldn't meet all her expenses, and last month, because she couldn't make rent, she got kicked out of her apartment and ended up on the street. Hearing this could well affect the young offender's sense of what the consequences of his actions actually were. This is the essence of restorative justice in practice.

Restorative justice is not possible without choosing the difficult path of finding alternatives to anger, righteousness, pride, and the rigid need to be right. This choice also requires a willingness to be open and present with our vulnerability. Tibetan popular wisdom says that anger is something we pick up when we feel weak because we think that it will make us feel strong. To assume a mantle of seeming strength, we use hostility, exclusion, and demonization.

Like forgiveness and reconciliation, restorative justice requires humility and the willingness of both victim and perpetrator to tear down the dividing wall between Us and Them. The illusion of separateness can only be maintained through denial: once we are humble enough to admit to ourselves that each of us contains "the seeds of all possible crimes," as a Quaker writer put it,[18] our grounds for feeling superior to others and contemptuous of their lives are removed. Self-righteousness erects a wall that truthfulness and clear seeing will always tear down.

Often we pay little attention to how our actions might ripple out into the world, but when we are reminded of how directly our behavior impacts others—both those we know and those we don't know—it can change our minds and hearts. A thought like, *It really doesn't matter what happens to them* changes to, *Actually it does matter, because they have the same needs and wants as I do. How would I like it if somebody took away my livelihood or harmed the people I love?* In the light of attention, our common ground expands.

Keeping after the Secret Enemy

Once we conquer the secret enemy of self-preoccupation by taking full responsibility for what happens to us, we have to keep at it moment by moment. Self-addiction and self-preoccupation are so firmly entrenched that we have to continually remind ourselves of the danger they pose and take steps to overcome them. For this we can repeat a prayer in the spirit of *The Blade Wheel of Mind Reform*, used to invoke our own fierce wisdom:

Smash, smash my self-preoccupation!
Love, love all-the-time other-preoccupation!

We affirm this notion and repeat the prayer again and again, applying it to all situations, one by one.

First, we remind ourselves how many lifetimes we have suffered through under the driving command of the secret enemies

---

18 Byron J. Rees, *The Heart Cry of Jesus* (1898) (Whitefish, MT: Kessinger Publishing, 2010), p. 17.

of self-addiction and self-preoccupation. In Buddhist cosmologies, the three most horrid states—or states of mind—are the hell realms, the hungry ghost realm, and the animal realm. The one we can most easily imagine is the animal state. Visualize yourself as a gazelle, with lions chasing you and eating you alive, taking huge bites out of your side or your thigh, or ripping your throat out, shaking you back and forth like a rag. Pretty soon the romantic, Bambi-like dream of being a gazelle fades.

When I was meditating on the misery of the horrid states for the first time, I got caught up in an image of Walt Disney's *The Living Desert*, which is one long pounce. The wasp is eaten by the tarantula, which is eaten by the snake, which is eaten by the hawk—someone is always creeping over the horizon and chomping on someone else. The Tibetans describe the animal state as "one eating another." The higher animals, closer to humans, have a little more leisure, but still they must be constantly vigilant, thus life is miserable for them.

Beneath the animal realm is the hungry ghost realm, where the beings have giant stomachs and throats as narrow as needles. They can swallow only one drop of fluid or one morsel at a time, so their stomachs constantly ache with hunger and their throats are parched with thirst. This is a state of utter craving and insatiable hunger and thirst.

The hell realms are even more frightening. There are freezing hells, boiling hells, crushing hells, and cutting hells, and the hell-beings are condemned forever to endure the most excruciating torment. Even with our vivid imaginations, however, we don't sufficiently fear these states. Certain that we will never be subjected to anything like the tortures of the damned, we continue to act in ways that bring us our own sorts of hell. But contemplating a Dantesque inferno would be a very good thing for us. Terror can be a stimulating force, inspiring us to take positive action to overcome destructive habits. For the Buddhist saint Milarepa, the terror he felt in thinking of his evil deeds was instrumental in propelling him toward enlightenment. Like the adrenaline rush that spurs you to jump out of the way of a speeding train, terror can be a powerful and useful spur to action.

As we gain insight into our self-addiction, we naturally become freer and more powerful. The confidence and contentment we project starts to attract the envy and adulation of others. It is crucial to keep wielding our wisdom blade against our self-preoccupation habit so that we do not succumb to the arrogance and pretensions of the spiritual adept. When you are tempted to think, *I am enlightened; I am special because I have invoked critical wisdom and gained insight into infinite life*, you must engage in mind reform and summon up other-preoccupation energy, the root of goodness. This is your defense against the secret enemy of self-habit and its buddy, self-preoccupation. The "I" in *I am special* reveals how deeply ingrained this habit is. But the wisdom of selflessness, intuition of the openness of total freedom as the reality of all things, brings us back to living in the world with an absolute concern for goodness.

So when we begin to coast on the laurels of our insight, with maximum ambition but minimum effort, we must summon the will to call on intuitive wisdom. *My* self-preoccupation; *my* self-obsession; *my* self-habit—self-preoccupation makes us weaker and weaker. We have to come to grips with how irrational we are when we are still in its thrall. We take friends too much for granted. Our greed for things is endless. In our frenzied commercial culture, we are whipped up by desire: *I can't live without this; I've got to have that.* Soon we are scheming to buy the world. And steal? Stealing is in people's minds everywhere and not just on a grand scale. Who hasn't fudged a little on their income tax? When we are under the spell of the devil of self-preoccupation, we fantasize about winning the lottery instead of thinking how we might earn a living in a way that would serve the world.

We human beings are skilled beguilers, artful in getting our way. We learn it as children: when a parent has something we want, we are ever so endearing. From a young age, we become adept at hinting for presents, flattering for favors, and stroking for recognition. However much we get, it is never enough, or it is too much of the wrong thing. We are perpetually dissatisfied. We cannot enjoy what we have or who we are with. Even lovers look over their shoulders, wondering if they made the wrong choice. We do as little as possible for others, and then we sit around complaining about how ungrateful they are and how little they do for us in return. This is just the way our minds work. Even in paradise we could manage to have a miserable time.

We use the blade wheel of mind reform to confront these personal habits. The "I" who calls on wisdom incarnate as Yamantaka, the Death-Exterminating wisdom, is the healthy, "real" person who challenges the bad behavior of the self-preoccupied "I," the enemy who habitually oppresses the living "I" who longs for liberation. That unreal "I," that never-satisfied, deceiving, false-construct "I," is the secret enemy we must continually go after with the blade wheel of selfless wisdom.

Dharmarakshita was highly enlightened, which enabled him to stay acutely aware of the persisting patterns of negative habits he should be alert to in his roles as a teacher and a human being. Though others usefully saw him as a guru, he still wanted to set an example of standing guard over the individual mind's instinctual propensity for egotism, lust, and hate. He calls himself out unsparingly:

In spite of my ideals, I'm stingier than a dog with his bone.
Although I might be bright, other-preoccupation, base of all virtue,
Still gets blown away by winds of self-preoccupying thoughts.
So, Death-Exterminating Wisdom, please,
Smash my lethal ego-thinker's head!
Terminate my secret enemy, my selfish heart.

Because I'm supposed to be holy and pure,
I'm not supposed to really love this or detest that.

So, I hide my loves and hates deep within.
I see only others as greedy or hating;
Then I scold them unfairly, and project my faults on them!
I haven't defused my own self-addiction,
So how can I complain about their faults?
So, Death-Exterminating wisdom, please,
Smash my lethal ego-thinker's head!
Terminate my secret enemy, my selfish heart.

Mindfulness brings us continuous awareness of the ongoing dangers of self-preoccupation and focuses on the need for transcendent wisdom. Once we have faced the evolutionary consequences inflicted by the demon of self-addiction, we embrace all adversity as atonement for bad deeds formerly committed under its spell. We then become motivated to cultivate the wisdom that is most powerfully represented by Yamantaka, the Death-Exterminator. We summon him with total determination to come to us at once and free us from our demon of self-preoccupation. We implore him to terminate our real innermost enemy, who defeats us by masquerading as our self and then constantly kills our natural life of freedom and happiness.

With your great compassion, save me from such
    downward evolution,
From foolish acts that power the wheel of desire.
I pray for you to triumph over my false self!
Conquer this negative self, deluded self,
Self-absolutizing self, megalomaniac self!
I implore you to triumph over it!

I cry out to you, glorious Yamantaka!
Take all possible miseries of life,
Not only my own but those of every being,
Pile them up on my self-addiction.
Let my self-obsession be the sacrifice

To liberate the real me, the selfless me!
My self-preoccupation, self-identity, destroys me—
Please load it up with the sufferings of all beings:
All bad thoughts, all addictions, the five poisons—
Delusion, lust, hatred, pride, and envy—
Pray, heap them on my self-impersonating demon!

This is where the teaching becomes what we would call homeopathic—using fire to fight fire, poison to fight poison. I see now how all evil comes out of self-obsession. Since I am still listening to my own words in my own mind, I ask Yamantaka to go into my unconscious, into the DNA of my spiritual makeup, with all his surgical tools, and destroy this habitual self-instinct, this voice of self-concern and self-obsession and self-promotion that I identify as my own.

Now, when I meditate on the kindness of all other beings, I can see that all other beings are trying to be kind to me, that they have no harmful intent toward me, that all the harm I experience is stimulated by my self-habit. I take upon myself all that is unwanted by others. I dedicate all my virtues to all other beings. And now, because of my vow to turn the static self inside-out, I can use all of the sins, the sufferings, the poisons of all other beings, and by wisdom transmute them into the medicine of enlightenment. When the demon of selfishness and self-centeredness is smashed by Yamantaka, finally we get the satisfying happiness that we have wanted all along.

And yet, is there still something lurking beneath the devil of self-instinct and self-preoccupation, some little flaw that mars our perfect enjoyment of nirvana here and now in the midst of ordinary life? At this point we come up against an even deeper, subtler level of self-addiction: the super-secret enemy.

DEATH, THE GREAT AWAKENER

Death, to most of us, is the greatest enemy of all. Nothing is more horrifying to card-carrying members of a materialist society than the reality that the physical body is doomed to die.

We view death not only as the enemy of the body but as the annihilator of meaning as well. Unlike other animals, humans are driven by the need for our lives to mean something. Given our hunger for significance, death is the adversary that wipes out any hope of eleventh-hour renown and reduces our lives to nothingness.

Buddhism does not view life and death in this reductive way. Rather than framing life as a losing battle in which the enemy of impermanence always wins, life and death are seen as inseparable processes with a sacred connection (think of the united opposites yin and yang). The promise of extinction enriches life if we allow it to, deepening gratitude for the preciousness of our human birth and bonding us, through compassion, to the rest of our mortal brothers and sisters.

Many spiritual traditions uphold this view. The notion that death can accentuate the meaning of life rather than annihilating our existence can turn this most feared enemy into an intimate friend, as close to us as our own shadow.

As a metaphor for the human condition, the Chinese sage Chuang Tzu told a story about a man who was so displeased with the sight of his shadow and the sound of his footsteps that he determined to get rid of both. The method this fearful man hit upon was to run away from his shadow, but with every step he took, the shadow naturally accompanied him without the slightest difficulty. The man concluded that he wasn't running fast enough, so he stepped up the pace, running faster and faster without stopping until finally he dropped dead. This poor man failed to realize that if he merely stepped into the shade, his shadow would vanish instantly. And if he sat down and stayed still, there would be no more footsteps.

The same principle applies to accepting our own death. When we step into the wisdom of impermanence, fear decreases proportionately. When we sit down and stay still, centering ourselves through mindfulness practice, the footsteps of panic begin to fade. Conscious of mortality, we live with greater care and gratitude; this awareness, in turn, makes way in the heart for lovingkindness. When we fully experience the moments of our lives, from their arising through experience to passing away, we learn to "die" in every moment in order to be reborn—to be awakened. Far from being our enemy, death is the great awakener. And the time for practicing acceptance of death is now, before the actual challenge of dying is upon us.

This is difficult practice, because most of us have trouble facing the fact that we will die. The mind is well defended against its own extinction. We resist the truth of the mortality of those we love, as well. The classic story of Kisa Gotami illustrates this resistance and the lengths we will go to with denial. Kisa Gotami was a wealthy man's wife who lost her only child. Desperate with sorrow, she was beyond consolation. Nobody could help this mother who seemed to have lost not only her beloved child but also her reason for living. Her sorrow was so great that many thought Kisa Gotami had lost her mind as she walked about with the corpse of her dead baby clutched in her arms. Finally, she consulted the Buddha: her only request was that he bring her child back to life. The Buddha told her that before he could bring the child back to life, she needed to procure a white mustard seed from every household in which no one had died.

Kisa Gotami went from house to house, but to her great disappointment, she could not find a single one where no member of the family had died. Finally it dawned on her that no house was free of mortality because it is the nature of human beings to die. Chastened, she returned to the Buddha, who comforted her and taught her about impermanence. Through this teaching, it is said that Kisa Gotami was awakened and entered the first stage of spiritual mastery. And she was finally able to bury her child.

From one perspective, it seems like a cruel way to teach her this all-important lesson. But the Buddha's initiation showed Kisa Gotami that she was not alone and that truth enlightened her. She was still a part of life, she realized. Her child had died but life continued, and part of that continuation lay in having compassion for other people who had suffered their own insupportable losses.

We renew ourselves by renewing the world and working to relieve the suffering of other people coping with illness, old age, and death. Learning to refocus our outrage toward death into compassionate action is not an easy practice. Viewed from one angle, life is completely unfair: how outrageous that just when we are getting the hang of living we are obliged to die. A recovering alcoholic once told me, "Goddamnit. I spent all this time and energy on getting sober and getting well psychologically, and then I got the diagnosis."

Yes, it's unfair that we should have to die. But it's a fact. What we do with our howl of outrage is the main point. My late friend the writer Rick Fields, poured some of his outrage into writing poetry, including one titled "Fuck you, Cancer."[19] Rick had recurrent metastatic lung cancer that he rallied against for many years, using both traditional and alternative medicines. He never tried to pretend that he was less angry than he was, which endowed him at the end with amazing grace. Rick talked about not making an enemy of his own death. What he meant is that death is often viewed in this culture as a kind of betrayal, something that should not be happening. This

---

19 In Rick Fields, *Fuck You Cancer and Other Poems* (New York: Crooked Cloud Projects, 1999).

denial is tied to the notion that we ought to be in control of everything; and death is a reminder that our body has somehow eluded our control, which leads us to conclude that something alien, something wrong, is taking place. Rick was defiant in standing up to death, but he never fell into the trap of hatred or the delusional belief that something mistaken was occurring in his dying body.

We import aggression into the unlikeliest of areas. Thirty or so years ago, when visualizations became popular as an adjunct to conventional cancer treatments, patients were encouraged to visualize their cancer cells as alien invaders and their immune system as a knight in armor slaughtering the cells. As video games became ubiquitous, the knight was replaced by a Pac-Man-like figure gobbling up enemy cells. That image worked well for some people, but others would come to me and say, "I can't do that. I need a less combative method." They weren't comfortable visualizing their ailing bodies as battlefields. Instead, they chose to use images of integration. Rather than seeing cancer as the enemy, they viewed it as a cell making an effort to live but in a way that was too much, too fast, and too invasive. In order to heal, these people needed to integrate their whole experience—the confusion, the anger, the fear and the times of joy and equanimity as well—so that they could have a more peaceable relationship with their lives than imagining themselves in a video game.

They needed to maintain the perspective that their life force had expressed itself through the cancer, and the cancer was an expression of their life force. In this way, they could see the cancer not as an enemy alien but as a terribly misguided and out-of-control part of themselves. This approach was not weak or self-defeating, an excuse for passivity or giving up, but rather a completely different way of relating to disease that was more empowering, in fact, than anything in the warrior model. We are so conditioned to think of strength as inherently aggressive that it takes a complete about-face to understand the force of love, kindness, and compassion.

The sharp edge between anger and grace is not easy to balance on. It is, however, the way to freedom. By wrenching control out of our hands, death becomes our great liberator. I recently sat with a friend a couple of weeks before she died. She was at home, and her hospital bed had been set up in the dining room. The door was open to the garden, letting in a gentle breeze and the sound of birdsong as her life ebbed away. She was floating in and out of consciousness and after a period of silence, turned to me somewhat distraught and said, "I have to move all my things across the street."

"What do you mean?" I asked her.

"It's complicated!" she said.

I didn't know what she was talking about and didn't know what to say. I told her how much people loved her, how much I loved her. An hour passed, and it finally struck me what "across the street" probably meant. "Remember when you told me you had to move all your things across the street, and that it was complicated?" I said. "Actually, you don't have to move all your things. You can go across the street without them. It will be okay." "Really?" she asked. "I'm sure," I told her.

Our tendency to cling to the stuff of this world pushes us to drag our things—physical possessions, emotional baggage, old assumptions, and habitual reactions—through every transition. It is hard to contemplate letting go, let alone letting go of absolutely everything, as we cross the street of mortality. No wonder we think of death as the enemy! Detaching is a complicated process. It can easily morph into apathy, disinterest, depression, or withdrawal and the refusal to feel. But detachment is not about refusing to feel or not caring or turning away from those you love. It is not about disconnecting from your own experience, whatever that is. Detachment is profoundly honest, grounded firmly in the truth of what is. By the time we reach this stage, we are beyond the need or desire for an agenda, we have no time or use for manipulating.

Detachment, like renunciation, is a form of honesty. If you have ever sat with the dying, you know that they often display a kind of brilliance, clarity, wisdom, and freedom that we almost never see in anyone else. Meeting people at the end of their lives who have done intensive spiritual practice can be inspiring. Francisco Varela, a Chilean scientist who was a founder of the Mind and Life Institute and a close friend of the Dalai Lama, demonstrated this with great beauty. In a wonderful documentary film called *Monte Grande*, Varela, a man whose life had been dedicated to integrating brain science with spiritual practice, talks about the liberating power of death. He was very, very ill, close to dying, when he was being filmed, and he looked as if he were made of light.

"It is an everyday reflection," Francisco said of the dying process, after many years of living with cancer. "Letting go from one moment to the next, letting go of distraction, letting go of the out-breath in order to breathe in again. This is considered an echo of the big letting go. Where we let go of everything, it's almost like seeing. It's not dropping something. It's seeing—and generosity. In death, we are practicing a kind of generosity and relinquishing. Not clutching. That's the process of letting go."

Seeing that conditions constantly change, and that anything with the nature to arise must pass away, brings us into the present moment. This means not being complacent in any way about having a tomorrow. Realizing that our days really are numbered and that they are going by very quickly generates a sense of spiritual urgency. It evokes not our old enemies of fear and panic but an intensity of purpose. When we really come close to that recognition, we need to understand it as a great opportunity, not an obstacle or a barrier. This enables us to devote more of ourselves, more completely, to our everyday lives and spiritual practice.

Before making any choice or decision, Tibet's great yogi Milarepa used to ask himself, "What would I do if this were my last day?" It's an amazing undertaking, shining a laserlike beam on your life and stripping away any pretense. Try it. I experimented with Milarepa's practice when I was living in India. For a month or so, I decided to ask myself his question frequently. I was shocked to discover what a difference it made. Making choices from this truthful perspective creates fearlessness toward whatever we encounter, endowing us with the strength to persevere even through great emotional and physical pain. Penetrating so deeply into our experience, we no longer defer or deflect or give up. Priorities are easier to set.

One of my students, Elesa Commerse, a meditation teacher and long-term cancer survivor, describes how this worked for her:

> The real turning point in how I viewed my journey came when my then-Shambhala meditation teacher, Vivian Sovinsky, told me to consider the mastectomy I was scheduled to have as "practice." That's right. "Practice." She said it was "practice in dying." She said I was fortunate to have this chance to practice for the ultimate death. You know, the Big Bang day nobody talks about. End of life. No more breathing. White sheet over the face. Swan song. Your loved ones go home crying, or dazed, or oh, so ready to read your will. Into the zippered blue vinyl body bag. Into the casket or the cremation pyre. Kaput. Finito. No more you, period. That's it. Bye-bye.
>
> The fact that Vivian wasn't joking caught me off guard. After three failed lumpectomies, here was this sweet, lovely soul, talking to me from the heart about looking forward to the fortunate opportunity of losing a cherished body part in order to practice dying. Was she nuts? But somehow it worked. From that point on, I saw my breast as a beautiful sacrifice that would teach me and help prepare me for the moment when I would have to, as Vivian Sovinsky put it, "surrender it all."

We do not know exactly how or when we will die, but we do know for certain that we will die. It really makes no sense, then, to make death our enemy. We would only be fighting a losing battle with the inevitable, diverting precious energy away from the opportunities that await us in every moment of the time that remains.

CHAPTER 4

Victory over the Super-secret Enemy

With the defeat of the outer, inner, and secret enemies, joy and bliss well up within us. We are able to see the real meaning and purpose of life. We have faith in the natural goodness of the universe. Now we identify with all beings—there is no separation between us, no self and other, no Us versus Them. We can proceed with full confidence in the potential to fully awaken.

But for all that, there is still a shadow clouding our bliss—a disparity between our contemplative vision of the ocean of freedom and our daily experience of the storms and seemingly endless conflicts of ordinary life. We have now encountered the super-secret enemy. How do we achieve victory over it? Or will there always be this discrepancy between inner and outer, between what we envision and what we can achieve?

When we look for the source of this super-secret enemy, we find it deep within. Whatever joy and bliss we are experiencing, an underlying concern remains: we view ourselves as so undeserving that we could not possibly experience the utter magnificence of profound reality. But who told us that we do not deserve true fulfillment, ecstatic bliss, the love of all, and the love from all? Why, at bottom, do we expect so little of life? The super-secret enemy is our persisting low self-esteem.

This sense of unworthiness, this self-deprecation, self-loathing, and self-abnegation, is based on a deeply ingrained inferiority complex drummed into us from childhood by a culture afflicted with fear and ignorance. This inferiority complex cripples out imagination, constrains our enthusiasm, and imprisons us in sadness and despair. Victory over this super-secret enemy, our fourth and final victory, is won by recovering the powerful energies previously controlled by anger and hatred—the energy of fire and illumination that dispels all shadows and the energy of water and flow previously bound up with desire, attachment, and greed—and wielding them anew with wisdom.

This is the province of Buddhist Tantra, known as the Diamond Vehicle (Vajrayana). Closely guarded as an esoteric realm in traditional Buddhist teachings, Tantra has been kept secret because victory over the super-secret enemy must be built on the previous three victories. According to my teacher Tara Tulku Rinpoche, wisdom is used initially to destroy the world of egocentric suffering, and then once that world has been destroyed and we have discovered the clear light of the freedom void, with its quiescent but infinite energy, wisdom can be redeployed as Tantra—literally the infinite "continuum" of life, wisdom, and love—to rebuild the world of love and compassion that is ideally suited to help others find freedom and bliss.

When we are secure in our ability to use patience to overcome anger and hatred, we no longer need to use pain and suffering as an opportunity to develop more patience. And when we overcome our self-habit, letting go of our sense of a fixed, separate self, we can rest in the awareness that there is no difference between the enemy—the one who injures—and the injury and the one who is injured. Once anger is conquered by tolerance, insight, and forgiveness, its furious fire is available to be used creatively by wisdom. The force that was so destructive is transformed into heroic energy.

SELF-LOATHING

One afternoon in Dharamsala, India, the Dalai Lama's headquarters in exile, I was at a conference with him along with a group of scientists and philosophers. The topic was healing emotions. This was interesting from the outset because, apparently, there is no word in Tibetan for emotions. In their tradition, we have mind-states and the like but nothing called emotions.

At one point, I asked the Dalai Lama, "Your Holiness, what do you think about self-loathing?" He looked confused. "What do you mean?" he asked. I proceeded to explain the self-loathing that is so prevalent in American culture, the sense of believing oneself to be unworthy; a person undeserving of love; a sinner; a lowly, neurotic creature. His Holiness still looked puzzled. *How could one hate oneself when we are all born with buddha-nature, he wondered? Could self-loathing be some kind of nervous disorder? Was it dangerous? Did it have the potential to make a person violent?*

His confusion revealed a cultural gap that I found fascinating. Without idealizing Asian culture, it can be observed that Easterners are seldom burdened by the common Western belief that underneath it all we are inherently, absolutely flawed. For Buddhists, there is a refuge to be found in a fundamental faith in the essential goodness of human beings, which creates a sense of possibility and potential.

In our culture, which emphasizes individualism, ambition, competition, perfectionism, and drive, too many of us become our own worst critics. Without a sense of our natural goodness, we perceive ourselves as souls in need of salvation and consumers in need of the next novelty in order to feel worthy, complete, and sufficient. In a desire-driven, competitive society like ours, a good life is too often defined by striving for what we don't have and pushing to become somebody *more*. Viewing ourselves as faulty, incomplete, and guilty of imperfection, we spend our lives in a desperate struggle to overcome the myth of *not good enough*. The defining myth of our culture, it has a Sisyphean quality: we are continually rolling the rock up the hill only to have it roll down again before we reach the top. Happiness is ever elusive. Chronic failure is the super-secret enemy in the land of flawed, self-aware creatures who long to be better.

Although cultural attitudes and discrimination play a large part in creating the problem of self-loathing, things can and do change. Just ask Khris Brown, who contributed to the book *It Gets Better*, a project designed to offer hope to lesbian, gay, bisexual, and transgendered youth who are being bullied. Though Brown was harassed mercilessly in high school, she now says, "I think that being the 'other'—including being bisexual, gay, transgendered, or whatever—is so incredibly valuable. It gives you a unique perspective on how to overcome the horrible things that people do to one another in the name of fear, in the name of what they think is religious righteousness. To go through all that and to survive it—without any malice toward those people, with love and forgiveness in your heart, and with acceptance of yourself—is the way to help heal the world."

At this point, our choice of how to interact with those who are suffering is no longer conditioned by our need to extract the material of our own development from the situation. There is no further self-interest involved, because now we are self-fulfilled, other-preoccupied, ecstatic, blissful, perfectly satisfied beings. We embody selflessness with compassion, reaching out to take away others' agony and pain, and exchanging it for bliss.

Again we turn to Shantideva, following his path of thought to the victory over our super-secret enemy. To get rid of our self-loathing, our self-deprecation, we must imagine that we can become fully aware of the deepest reality of the free void and its infinite energy, the actual matrix of life and death, and make ourselves a fount of that enlightening energy.

We now turn our attention to universal compassion. We begin by contemplating the total equality of others and ourselves: We want pleasure and don't want pain; others want the same. We seek freedom and bliss; others seek the same. We are all equal in what we want, where we want to be, and where we want to go. Physically, we differ from one another; but we are all the same in not wanting to be hurt, not wanting to feel pain. So naturally we would want to be as protective of others as we are of ourselves.

"But wait a minute," you might say. "Other people's arms and legs are connected to *their* bodies, not to mine, and vice versa, so I don't *literally* feel their pain, nor do they feel mine. Why should I be as protective of them as I am of myself?"

The short answer is that the feeling of identity is not that mechanical. I only feel my own pain because I am programmed to identify it as mine. I could be hypnotized to ignore a burn; I could be asleep when a mosquito bites me; I could be intent on making a goal when someone kicks me—and in every case, I would not be identifying with the pain at that moment. So even feeling my own pain has a learned element in it. As that is so, I can also learn to feel the pains of others, to truly empathize with them. And when I empathize with them, I feel their pain deeply, and my compassion makes me try to keep them from experiencing further hurt.

Since we are all alike in wanting pleasure and hating pain, why should I favor myself over others? What is so special about me that I am the one who should be happy? What is so special about me that I should protect myself from pain but neglect other people? If I protect myself against pain that I infer I will feel in the future, why shouldn't I also protect others against pain that they may feel? If I imagine only my own pain, it is the self-habit at work again, underpinning the self-preoccupation that cuts off my compassion. I need to free myself of concepts that shut me off from feeling and reacting naturally to any pain, whoever is experiencing it.

We could be forgiven for thinking that if we feel others' pain it will increase the amount we suffer. But this is a moot point. For when we are clear about our interconnection with all beings, we see that we are already suffering the pains of others, often subliminally, as feelings of anxiety or dread or guilt or concern about not fulfilling our responsibility toward them. Compassion acknowledges our connection, our awareness that it is futile to deny our interrelatedness. It is our courageous outreach toward the wave of immense suffering experienced by other beings. Compassion gives us energy to bear all the suffering and do something to lessen it wherever possible. It allows us to move toward, not away from, pain. We know we are able to voluntarily endure pain in order to gain something greater, whether that something greater is strength, resilience, or pleasure. So if we voluntarily share the pain of others for the sake of a stronger connection to them or the pleasure of seeing their relief, what more could we wish for? Compassion, the wish to free others from suffering, is what frees us from suffering. The first person the compassionate person frees from suffering is herself.

SELF-ESTEEM VERSUS SELF-COMPASSION

Psychologists make a distinction between self-esteem and self-compassion. They point out that self-esteem depends on an impression of having succeeded, measured against objective standards (Am I good enough? Smart enough? Rich enough?), while self-compassion is unconditional open-heartedness that is self-sustaining through good times and bad. Self-esteem implies competitiveness and easily forsakes us when the chips are down.

According to psychologist Kristin Neff, self-compassion has three main components. The first is *self-kindness*, which means cutting ourselves some slack when we fall short of our own expectations. Rather than berating ourselves, we acknowledge that imperfection, failure, and painful difficulties are inevitable in life. Self-compassionate people understand that gentleness is more helpful than anger when we cannot meet our own ideals.

The second component of self-compassion is awareness of our *common humanity*. Much of why we suffer in the face of our internal enemies comes from a deep sense of isolation. We imagine that we are the only ones being disappointed or making mistakes. But self-compassion requires us to recognize that imperfection is a condition we share with every human being, though it is influenced by external factors such as genes, environment, and parenting. Recognizing our interconnection allows us to be less judgmental of falling short.

The third aspect of self-compassion is *mindfulness*. When we are aware of our negative emotions, we can regain equilibrium if we see our experiences in the larger context of human struggle. Mindfulness brings with it the willingness to observe feelings and thoughts as they are without trying to change or deny or ignore them. As Neff explains on her website, "We cannot ignore our pain and feel compassion for it at the same time."

Self-compassion teaches us that when we make mistakes we have a choice about how we treat ourselves afterward. Do we heap judgment and blame on ourselves, identifying completely with the error? ("You're so stupid for doing that stupid thing!") Or can we use suffering as a poignant reminder of human frailty? ("I thought it would get me what I wanted, but I was wrong. I was coming from a place where I knew so much less than I know now. How sad is that?") The difference is clear. Judgment is monolithic and near-sighted. Compassion is complex and expansive, an evolving part of a living system. It accommodates the reality that we operate with limited information and personal imperfection in nearly every moment of the day.

Men and women whom we call heroes, who have undergone great suffering or hardship or danger in order to save others, often describe the ecstasy they feel upon having rescued someone. That kind of other-preoccupied action goes beyond fear. Of course, we may not be able to be so self-sacrificing right off the bat. We can drown trying to save someone if we lack sufficient lifesaving skills. The wiser course is to work up to selfless action bit by bit. But if we can reach a place where nothing frightens us, where we are ready to face any danger and throw ourselves into it with full heroic abandon, we will surely feel great relief even in less dramatic situations. Always beckoning is our destination, the great ocean of bliss of enlightenment. And we can only enjoy real freedom when it is shared with others. What freedom could there be if we were shut off from our fellow beings? That would be tantamount to being imprisoned in solitary confinement.

Compassion is above all realistic. Altruism is not some impossible ideal. It comes of squarely confronting the truth of our interconnectedness. It therefore expands our approach to life by making us see that the pain of others is just as important as our own. It might even be argued that because there are so many more others than myself, they are more important than I am.

Why should I not identify with the bodies and lives and minds of others as if they were my own? That is exactly what we have to do in order to develop a more compassionate attitude. It is easy to see how harmful it is to be mired in the habit of self-regard. Stuck on myself, I miss so much: I fail to grasp what others want or how they feel; I feel lonely and neglected. When I am enclosed in my own bubble of self-preoccupation, very little that is positive can happen to me. But if I move to a more cosmic perspective and become aware of my shortcomings, I can see that their causes lie in my actions, not just in my genes, and I realize that my self-preoccupation habit has been causing me suffering forever. When I deeply acknowledge that, the world opens up.

And what a different world it is when, bit by bit, I switch my focus toward others and their wants and needs. I see how alienated and hopeless many of them feel, and I become engaged in the challenge of reaching out to them to pop the bubble of their self-preoccupation so that they can feel a connection to me.

When others sense my attention, my concern for them, they may react in all sorts of ways. Some are happily surprised; some are frightened; some are suspicious; some are tentatively receptive. As I pop more bubbles of self-preoccupation, I realize the challenges of connecting with other people. There is great skill involved in reaching out appropriately, and a kind of clairvoyance is needed to anticipate how they will perceive my concern, my speech, my body language.

There is a whole educational process involved in becoming compassionate. The first step is to develop sincere motivation, based on a sense of our unending connection to everyone. Once we embark on this educational process, we are saved from feeling self-congratulatory about our altruistic outlook by realizing that we are simply cultivating a habit. The more we focus on others, the more expanded our sense of being becomes and the more cheerful and uplifted we feel. We stop expecting others to make a fuss over us or reward us for our attention. Preoccupation with the fate of others becomes routine. And just as in caring for a child we become alert to her every movement in order to keep her from injuring herself, attending carefully to others is aimed at making sure they do not hurt themselves.

Since there are so many distractions when we are interacting with others, at first it may be hard to pay such close attention to them. Therefore, the education in altruism requires us to practice various contemplative exercises to help us become more sensitive to other people so we can identify with them closely and be more accurate about what they need and want.

Putting Ourselves in Another's Shoes

Bit by bit, we can experiment with feeling what it is like to "put ourselves into the other fellow's shoes," being careful not to show off to them what we are doing, lest they find our attention invasive. How amazing and exciting it is to "be" another person, even remotely—to imagine yourself as the other person so that you feel their perceptions as your own. This kind of imaginative projection helps us see other people's points of view, whether we agree with them or not. And we can expand the experiment so that we imagine being several people at once, perhaps quietly watching from a distance as two people are interacting, and imagining how first one and then the other is feeling as they become attuned to each other.

This is how the great bodhisattvas of Buddhist legend experienced the world, their consciousness so open to connection with others that they could feel themselves alive in every being. For us, that infinite awareness manifests as whatever it takes to embrace others with love and compassion, and turn them toward awareness of their own freedom and happiness and away from what they habitually experience as limitation and suffering.

The bodhisattva Avalokiteshvara, who is believed to be incarnated in the present Dalai Lama, represents the infinite altruism of enlightened beings. It is said that Avalokiteshvara made a solemn vow that anyone who heard his name, just by hearing it, would begin to feel that they, too, could find freedom and happiness. Upon becoming a monk, Shantideva chose his own Dharma name, Sanskrit for "God of Peace," so that anyone hearing it would feel peaceful. The name Christ comes from the Greek *christos*, meaning "anointed," anointed by the grace of a compassionate God.

To whatever degree we can expand our sense of identity to include others and preoccupy ourselves with their condition, to that degree we will be happier ourselves. Therefore, we should practice the exchange of self and others, in which we exchange self-preoccupation for other-preoccupation. (See Appendix, page 166, for a visualization practice of give and take, which is related to the exchange of self and other.)

To truly switch self-preoccupation for other-preoccupation, we work up to giving even our body and our life for the sake of others, if necessary. Practically speaking, what this means is that bit by bit, we work on diminishing an exaggerated attachment to the body. If I did not perceive my body as so delicate, so vulnerable, I would not be so afraid of small discomforts and pains. So I need to become less attached to my body. And I must no longer take the lives of other beings to feed it or commit any sort of violence to defend it.

Our bodies can get us into a lot of trouble. Therefore, our attachment to the body itself can be our enemy. This is super-secret to most of us, however, so we must be careful not to take the statement "My attachment to my body is my enemy" literally and harm ourselves as a result. We are not talking about destroying the body but about using it properly, as a gift. This can be an important part of exchanging self for other, so our goal in developing greater altruism is served by becoming less and less attached to the body. And we certainly will not be attached to the body if we develop the secret vision that sees such attachment as an enemy. Let me clarify: just as preoccupation with the self is destructive to the self and pre-occupation with others benefits the self, so body-obsession, narcissism, and vanity are actually harmful to the body. The hypochondriac worries about getting sick all the time and as a result becomes sick more often than someone who is less obsessed with the body's every twinge. The young girl who compares herself ceaselessly to fashion models becomes afraid to eat and develops anorexia or bulimia, seriously endangering her life. The narcissistic person spends hours and thousands of dollars fussing over his appearance to the detriment of healthy self-regard.

Dancing, exercise, movement practices, and playing sports are less self-obsessed ways of honoring the body, and people with a positive attitude toward the body and a respectful understanding of how to maintain its health are more likely to thrive. This is yet another of life's paradoxes: the less preoccupied with our bodies we are, the better we fare.

In the practice of exchanging self and other, paradoxes abound. For example, when we are about to give away something we really like—give a scarf to a friend who admired it, for example—we are sometimes stopped by the thought, *If I give this away, I won't be able to enjoy it later.* But this sort of thinking leads to miserliness. Holding on to things because they might be useful later ends up imprisoning us under piles of useless stuff. Have you ever seen one of those TV reality shows about hoarding? Far from enjoying their accumulated things, the hoarders are depressed, isolated from family and friends, and literally buried alive. A pile of gold bullion hidden away in a bank vault has no practical value. Even a huge bank account is just a bunch of numbers on a piece of paper unless you put it toward something good: invest it, give it to worthy causes, or use it to support opportunities in your life. People who practice exchanging self and other tend to be conscious consumers, not conspicuous consumers. When they are about to spend money on nonessentials, they are often stopped by the thought, *Will*

I really enjoy this when I could be using the money to help someone else instead? This attitude is the opposite of the miser's. It is the thriftiness of the truly generous.

When we are lost in our self-preoccupation, we focus on what gives us an advantage over others, not realizing that self-preoccupation creates a momentum that can lead to unpleasant consequences in the future. Even a little self-sacrifice enables us to do much good for others. We need to develop the evolutionary perspective that the biological theory of karma encourages, a long view that extends beyond this moment or even this lifetime. While we should take care not to deprive ourselves to the point of risking our own or our dependents' survival, we can also recognize that a little self-sacrifice in the service of others moves us toward the supreme benefit of becoming enlightened, of awakening to true happiness and universal love.

When you live an evolutionary life, you understand causality in a way that is very different from how it is seen by someone who has only this lifetime in mind. You no longer grab what you can get right now, heedless of the consequences. If you manipulate others, using them for your own purposes, the karmic worldview implies that in your evolutionary future you will end up as a slave to others. But when you serve others, using yourself for their benefit, you become the master of the universe. I think of this way of being as "the Shantideva Challenge."

The Shantideva Challenge

Shantideva declared that all happiness in the world comes from wishing for the happiness of others—that is to say, it comes from love. And all misery in the world comes from wishing for our own happiness—that is to say, it comes from selfishness. This, of course, runs counter to conventional wisdom. But it does not take much to awaken us to the fact that our dissatisfaction with what we have and our insatiable need for more are self-defeating—guaranteed to result in relationship difficulties, problems at work, and disappointment at home.

Every year I challenge students in my college classes to tell me a happiness they enjoyed that resulted from seeking their own happiness. They cite different experiences—the guys invariably cite sex—but when we analyze those experiences, we almost always find that the real key to their happiness is that they forgot about seeking their own happiness and lost themselves in the experience, always in relationship to others, directly or indirectly.

Self-involved people, locked inside with their concern for themselves and thinking about what they have, what they don't have, what they want—how dissatisfied they are, in other words—are really dead to the world. They cannot punch their way out of the paper bag of their own self-involvement. Unable to connect with others or focus on how others perceive them, they live in isolation, no matter how big the crowd around them. An altruistic person, on the other hand, focuses on what others want and need, and how to help them get it so they will be happy. While the isolated person ends up in a hell of alienation, the enlightened person is in bliss.

When I practice exchanging my self-preoccupation for other-preoccupation, I am already making a significant advance in evolutionary progress, a step toward greater being. The more I take on the suffering of others and share my own happiness with them—using the meditation of give and take and the daily practice of the exchange of self and other that subdue the secret self—the more expansive I become. As I experience life from the perspective of others, my own life opens up to the world. Parents coming to the aid of their children find so much power in their efforts because they are acting for the sake of their family, expanding their identification with the group. Teammates do that, too, and so do lovers. But if we fail to expand our awareness and identify with others, we stay stuck in our self-addiction and cannot evolve as spiritual beings or even increase our worldly happiness by improving our relationships with those around us.

Realistically, the self-preoccupied person's prospects in life are limited. If we carry on with our selfish ways, people will not like us. People who serve us in some way will do so grudgingly and ineffectively; and those we serve will fail to appreciate our service, since it is given grudgingly and ineffectively. Not only will we be ineffective in our relationships with others, but we may actually harm people, because we do not consider the effect of our actions. The self-habit sets up a lose-lose situation, so that our aim to thrive and prosper in this life is doomed to failure.

When we look at the world around us, we can see all the violence that results from trying to get what we think will make us happy and get rid of whatever we think stands in the way. The self-preoccupation of each participant in this deadly dance is clearly the source of this violence and pain. If every individual, every country, every group, could just see the other's point of view—and realize that sometimes it is better than our own, or that with a little effort the two views could co-exist or even harmonize—much of the violence in the world today could be avoided. The self-preoccupation habit, the rigid-identity habit, is the real enemy plaguing the world. Only by letting go of self-concern and turning all our attention to others and their concerns can we get rid of this enemy. We need to wholeheartedly affirm:

> I am here for others. They are my only purpose in life. I am like the mother of a newborn, worrying about what my child wants and needs. I concentrate on looking at life through the others' eyes. I give up looking around for what I want. Everything I have, even my body, I place at the service of others. I will not misappropriate it for my own purposes.

Now, when we see others, we are at the same time seeing ourselves as they see us. So we can begin to modify our relationship with them for the better. Our habitual way of looking at other people is to judge them. Either they are one up on us, or we are one up on them, or we are equal. When someone is one up on us, we feel jealous. When we are one up on them, we feel condescending. When we feel we are equal, we become competitive, seeing others as rivals. So now, when we look at ourselves through their eyes, we feel the reverse. This tendency to judge is spontaneous and subliminal, but once we are empathic with others, we recognize that as we are judging them, they in turn are judging us. Seeing through their eyes, we feel what it is like to be judged.

This is the heart of the equalizing yoga, the exchange of self and other (similar to the give and take meditation but rather a living yoga practiced all the time, both meditating and acting in the world). Through this practice we open our boundaries to join the community. We change our energy source from self-preoccupied egotism to empathic compassion. We gradually expand our self-identity to include more and more others. We embark upon this journey to bring happiness to the whole world, rising up heroically to assume responsibility for all beings. Creative imagination becomes our primary instrument, now that we have taken it back from the lowly role it served in maintaining our habitual, self-preoccupied worldview.

Embracing an Infinite Lifestyle

When we have risen to the Shantideva challenge, we automatically feel the invitation to embrace the total interconnection with all beings that flows from exchanging self-preoccupation for other-preoccupation—a process that parallels what I call "breaking free from the terminal lifestyle and adopting the infinite lifestyle." While this infinite perspective is universally beneficial, the invitation to adopt it cannot be accepted too prematurely. Before we take on the embrace, since we are, ultimately, realistic beings, we must understand the inevitability of some form of infinite continuum of relative selves and relative others. In other words, we have to break free from our conviction that this lifetime is all there is; that our present body-mind is all we will ever be; and that we therefore need to worry about ourselves and our loved ones only up until our death, because when our body gives out, we will be gone forever, no matter how good or bad we have been. Deeply understanding the overwhelming probability that the mental energy of our consciousness will continue after the death of this body frees us from our terminal lifestyle and automatically commits us to the infinite lifestyle. In this way, entering into the infinite lifestyle with a view to optimizing it for yourself and your dear ones, however small or large your circle of love may be, is not a leap into the beyond, a gamble, a dangerous experiment. Rather it is a practical step, realistic and commonsensical, that makes the best of a sure thing.

This view has an implication, however, that is bound to be daunting at first, so it is optional and not forced on anyone. We should not be overly enthusiastic and try to embrace that implication prematurely, only to fall back in discouragement and become cynical. We embrace infinite life through endless lifetimes on the simple premise that if life is infinite and death nothing but a swift transition from one life to another, then we have always been living and will always continue to live. The big question then becomes: *How* will we live? Will it be in happiness or sorrow? What can we do to ensure our future happiness and avoid future sorrow? When we become aware that we live in the context of the infinite consequences of everything we think, say, or do, we vastly improve our chances of finding happiness, since we immeasurably intensify our loving care for ourselves and others.

The further implication of this infinite-life context is that all living beings are just the same as us. All of them have been living beginninglessly, just like us, and will continue to live endlessly, just like us. We have had infinite chances of engaging with them an infinite number of times, as they have had with us. And we have been, and will remain, infinitely engaged with all of them.

Our historical Shakyamuni Buddha, in all accounts of his enlightenment under the bodhi tree, is said to have first remembered all his infinite previous lives and then to have become aware of the previous lives and future destinations of all other beings. As his awareness expanded infinitely with his enlightenment, he viscerally experienced his infinite intertwinement with all beings.

Though we are not yet viscerally aware of it, we have all been everything to one another in past lives—mother, father, lover, child, teacher, ally, rival, enemy—and we will continue to be everything to one another in future ones. Therefore, for our infinite living to become infinite happiness, others must experience their infinite living as infinite happiness. So even though we have not yet fully experienced the infinite bliss of awakening, we naturally decide that we will awaken the whole world of beings along with us.

Once we know this, our motivation is no longer just to liberate ourselves from suffering. We recognize that it would be impossible to experience perfect bliss if even one single being had no share in it and continued to suffer. The Buddha taught that this powerful desire to deliver all beings from suffering is the very soul of awakening, the soul of the bodhisattva, who is dedicated to saving the world. The soul of awakening is aware of its oneness with all other souls, intermittently at first, needing reminders. But eventually this awareness becomes its natural orientation. It is the soul of one who is determined to save the whole community from suffering and considers all beings the community.

NO MORE SELF-HATRED

A student of mine named Tracy told me how she freed herself from chronic self-hatred by paying attention to her internal monologue: "One of the biggest things for me has always been wanting things to be different. I grew up in an abusive home and continued to be abused in adulthood by a violent partner.

"I was constantly thinking, *I'm not good enough, not worthy. I deserve nothing. Who would love me?* Finally, the pain was so much that I just shut down."

Years went by before Tracy somehow made her way to a psychiatrist. "I had no idea how angry I was," she recalls. "My heart was locked down tight." At her therapist's suggestion she agreed to try meditation. She sat and followed her breath, noting the stories she kept rehashing in her head. "Meditation has transformed my life," she says now. "When my story comes through—*I'm not good enough*—and I start feeling anxious, I can breathe and bring myself back to the present moment, knowing the thoughts will pass. I am learning about impermanence. Pain passes. I can sit with it. It is so liberating."

She continues, "Right at this moment I can feel the sadness, the grief in my chest. But it is different. It is just sadness. I can be with it with an open heart and let it go. And, a huge thing for me—I have been able to hold my own self in lovingkindess . . . although that is a work in progress! It is not perfect . . . and it is not always easy . . . but I can do it."

The confidence of knowing that freedom is possible in the face of our demons gives us strength when they threaten to beat us down. Knowing that we can make different choices, decide on new paths, aim our mind toward something bigger, and sustain our vision no matter what comes up, reminds us that we always have a source of light, whatever dark room we may enter.

Victory over the Super-secret Enemy

Now, having overwhelmed the super-secret enemy with the magnificent vision of the bodhisattva, we can seal this victory with a positive visualization. Here in the realm of wisdom and compassion, the energy wielded so destructively by anger is freed for creative use. My teacher Tara Tulku said that the energies that make up the world of suffering—delusion, pride, stinginess, lust, greed, envy, and anger—are all destroyed by wisdom. Delusion, or ignorance, is the root of them all, since they all depend on maintaining the notion of Us versus Them, of a fixed self separate from other fixed selves. When this delusion is finally destroyed, wisdom can reappropriate these destructive energies to rebuild a world of freedom and bliss.

Anger's explosive energy becomes pure wisdom, which fells all obstructions, dissects all resistance to freedom, and consumes death and life in the infinitely free voidness of relativity. Hatred energy transmuted into ultimate-reality-perfection wisdom is like a gentle, life-giving nuclear explosion, blasting away the confusion. This kind of realization can lead to the transformation of the environment and society, the turning of the ego-universe of suffering into the buddha-verse of free and loving individuals within supportive communities.

In the Time-Machine (Kalachakra) Tantra, it is said that more than 2,000 years ago in the magical hidden kingdom of Shambhala, King Yashas, an emanation of the wisdom bodhisattva Manjushri, abolished the caste system and proclaimed the total equality of all citizens. He announced that from that time on, every person would belong to what he called the *vajra* class, i.e. the diamond class. This proclamation meant that everyone would possess a share of royal power. In other words, everyone would be, to some extent, a king or queen. This universally shared symbolic kingship resonates powerfully with our precious ideal of democracy, in which every citizen has authority and helps to decide the leadership and law of the land. At the heart of Thomas Paine's influential pamphlet *Common Sense*, which argued for independence from British rule, is a powerful image of the American Revolution as the shattering of the royal crown of the king, and democracy as the return of the crown jewel fragments to the citizens of the land, with each owning one of the jewels, signifying the sovereignty of the people.[20] In our effort to overcome our super-secret enemy of self-loathing, it is important to question the idea much drummed into us that society is always oppressive and humans can never get along, that each one will always be out for himself, and that it is ultimately a tensely controlled Hobbesian realm of war of all against all. Just as we are potentially blissful, free, loving, and beloved beings, so our planetary society can be a supportive and fulfilling environment in which we all can flourish together.

NO MORE ENEMIES

Generosity breaks down the Us-versus-Them divide. It acknowledges our shared human bond. In one of the Buddha's discourses, he instructed a king on enlightened leadership: "To be a good leader, you have to be just and generous." The king was just, but he neglected being generous, with the result that his people were going hungry. Because they were hungry, they had started stealing, and because they were stealing, the king had begun to build more jails. What should he do? the king asked. "You forgot something basic," the Buddha said. "If you don't want people to steal, be generous. Give them food."

Generosity goes hand and hand with lovingkindness, because in that moment of giving we feel goodwill toward those who are receiving; we feel a sense of

---

20   Thomas Paine, *Common Sense* (1776) (Mineola, NY: Dover Publications, 1997), pp. 31–32.

oneness with them, rather than alienation from them. Generosity goes hand in hand with compassion when we realize that nothing happens in isolation and that we are all responsible for the well-being of one another. Generosity goes hand in hand with sympathetic joy as we rejoice in the happiness of the recipient rather than feeling somehow impoverished or diminished because of our offering. Generosity goes hand in hand with equanimity, as we are willing to let go of our possessions without resistance or regret.

Tenderhearted concern for others does not mean being foolish. For compassion to be real, it must be paired with wisdom. Charity runs the risk of patronizing the recipient, subtly setting up a one-up, one-down relationship that perpetuates feelings of separation. We need to understand the great web of interconnection, and then we will be moved to help out of our awareness that we are all in this life together. When we have overcome our enemies, inner and outer, we practice generosity as an outpouring of the happiness we have found.

Good leaders—wise kings and queens—have a responsibility to rule well, to do what is right and best for all their people. Frequently, we entertain secret fantasies about being powerful and think that we are working hard to succeed. But actually, we fear real power and the responsibilities it carries. One of our most comforting delusions is that we have no power and therefore what we do, say, and think does not really matter. But we need to overcome this delusion and accept responsibility for our contribution to our own and others' lives. We need to develop the deeper kind of stable self-confidence that is free of the self-inflation and self-promotion that arise out of a basic feeling of insecurity.

The Yoga of Self-Creation

One of the logical implications of selflessness, the voidness, relativity, and hence fluidity of our identities, is that our self is always changing and that we are responsible for being creative about ourselves as works in progress. If we are all going to be wise rulers of our own lives and inspiring examples for others, we need a practice to help prepare us for our critical role. In the magical country of Shambhala, the people regularly practiced the unexcelled Tantric yoga of self-creation. The king was a supreme adept of this technology and conducted spiritual initiations and coronation rituals in the gardens outside his royal palace, helping each person in the realm to envision himself or herself as the king or queen of his or her own buddha-verse. Although we may not live in Shambhala, each of us has to take responsibility for the fragment of the royal crown we have been given, and create our own enlightened kingdom.

The yoga of self-creation begins with a mantra:

Come to me, divine energy! I am the one whose real nature is the diamond, the intuitive knowledge of freedom![21]

Try saying these sentences out loud. They are quite powerful. With this mantra, you let go of your habitual sense of self. You let your body and mind dissolve down through the darkness of unconsciousness and into the realm of clear light. You affirm the foundation of your being in the absolute knowledge of selflessness. You surrender any hold you have on being or owning anything. You let go of all words and thoughts, forms, sounds, smells, tastes, and textures. You abandon even the sense of sinking into the absence of these things. Here you find infinite life. You are filled with the power of your true self, your bodhisattva soul of universal good. You are present with,

---

21   om shunyata jñana vajra svabhava atmako aham.

and inseparable from, the deepest hearts of all buddhas, gods, goddesses, humans, and other beings throughout the universe. You experience the energy of total bliss.

As you continue with self-creation yoga, it is crucial that you maintain this sense of boundless existence, which is absolutely secure in its groundlessness. In the vast and energetic peacefulness of selflessness, you do not feel isolated in some realm outside of relationships with other beings. On the contrary, you enfold all beings, including those you know, those you have never known, and those you can only imagine. You joyously and lovingly consider every single cell and every single thought of every single being, seeing all beings as no different from you. You recognize that most people delude themselves, and your universal compassion moves you to help them all feel the freedom and bliss that they deserve to feel. The more powerful your empathy becomes, the more intense is your will to provide for others' happiness.

Conventional actions seem too slow and inadequate. For your love to accomplish its will, you will need a higher technology. Tapping into the creativity usually bound up in idle fantasizing, you envision the world as a place of beauty and security, a sacred and exquisite place free from suffering. You see yourself as a fount of wisdom, overflowing with perfect love and goodness.

You shape your universe however you wish, visualizing it as elements of energy—wind, fire, water, and earth—arising out of the spacious free void. You stabilize those elements in a cosmic pattern that feels secure to you and surround it with an impenetrable force field of protection. You bring all beings together in a place that is perfect for coping with their needs, in human bodies that express their stage of evolution perfectly, each one enjoying their highest potential.

You are not a concrete embodiment separate from them but rather an all-encompassing cloudlike awareness that enfolds the entire world and all the vast streams of beings as a maternal or paternal presence that feels boundless love and compassion for each of these beings. They are cradled in your energy of bliss, suffused with your sustaining wisdom and compassion. You do not ignore their suffering, physical and mental, as they struggle against one another and a world they fear. You realize how each person perceives the world outside of them as Other, and your loving concern is automatically reflected to them as whatever will best put them at ease, open them up, and make them wish to connect to others in a positive way. You are a vast teaching machine that gives itself wholly to everyone.

Visualize yourself in whatever way will best respond to the needs of the individuals with whom you wish to interact. Whatever the sex of your normal body, visualize yourself as male if that is the best way to approach a specific person, or female if that would be the better way. Whether your skin is black, white, yellow, red, or brown, visualize yourself as a member of whatever race can best relate to a particular person or situation. Though you are human, visualize yourself as an animal if a certain species would be less threatening to someone. If, for example, you are approaching a frightening, evil person who would meet your normal human form with great hostility, imagine approaching this person as a cat or dog or horse or camel and see the person petting you, momentarily letting down their guard to embrace your gentle form.

Combine these visualizations with the constant practice of exchanging self and other. Note people whom you usually look down on, however subtly, and look at your normal self through their eyes: feel how they sense your condescension and respond with envy and resentment. Be aware of how you look to them as you move, gesture, speak, and stand in their presence. See them as they see you, through the green eyes of envy and unease. Try to move your awareness completely out of yourself, and be present empathically within the other.

Once you succeed in this act of imagination, chose a different person, someone you normally consider a rival in some respect and regard warily, competitively, looking for their weakness and an opportunity to take advantage of them. Regard yourself through their eyes with that same unease, fear, competitiveness, and aggressiveness. Again, try to get out of yourself and totally into the other person's awareness.

When you have experienced this person, choose a third person whom you normally regard as higher than you in some way, someone you look up to with admiration mixed with jealousy and resentment, who normally might look at you, however subtly, with condescension or even contempt. See yourself as that person sees you.

As you become adept at imaginative empathizing, you can practice it while going about your ordinary day. When you see someone on a bus, in a restaurant, or on TV, imagine you are that person, seeing you from their perspective. As your empathic radar becomes more and more attuned, you will feel yourself becoming much less self-preoccupied and much more aware of your impact on others. You will be much more attuned to their happiness.

Whenever you become overwhelmed by how vast the suffering of beings seems to be, you can dissolve your sense of yourself as normal and ordinary, and visualize yourself as the Diamond-Force Time-Machine Buddha, a deep blue being with supreme self-confidence and total commitment to the immediate happiness of all beings. As you rest in this sense of buddha-identity, you do not have to think about your virtue, power, insight, and energy, because you embody them all absolutely. You are invulnerable in the face of terror, pain, and death. You are time itself, not only manifesting in the here and now but also infinitely present throughout time and space. All beings sense your existence. Even those who feel stuck in a horrible life find hope when they see you: you assure them of future relief from their suffering. You feel immense compassion for every individual, and your desire for their happiness holds enormous transformational potential. All beings look to you for guidance and security as they journey through the ups and downs of life. You tolerate no misery or meanness. Evil beings melt into goodness at the sight of you.

Imagine yourself in a giant palace, like the Taj Mahal, standing in the center of a magnificent garden filled with gods and goddesses dancing in endless, exquisite bliss. You draw all beings toward this blissful place, establishing each of them in the most exalted situation imaginable. You feel ecstatic joy as these beings overcome their delusions, fear, pain, and anxiety, and relax into peace and joy. They then return to their ordinary environment feeling contented, virtuous, and benevolent—a source of help and happiness to others. Using the methods you have modeled, all people begin working to create an enlightened self and enlightened societies, until they, too, radiate wisdom and bliss.

Continue your meditation from within this feeling of ecstasy, this architecture of sublime power and connectedness, as you joyously survey the universe. Your body is interconnected with the bodies of all enlightened beings who have ever been, including all the deities of every culture on the planet, of all times. You resonate with them all, and then you send them out to purify the environment, to bring relief to all beings. This is you as the Diamond-Force Time-Machine Buddha.

When you feel restored, filled with the energy and determination to realize this magical vision, you can begin to slowly dissolve in stages from your enormous blue body of many faces and arms, back into your subtle, selfless essence. You then arise from the meditation in your normal body, returning to ordinary life in your habitual circumstances. But now you have the knowledge that you are indivisible from the Diamond-Force Time-Machine Buddha. The security and power you have discovered remain within you, alive and active, sources of inspiration and self-respect that allows you to go forth to change the world and yourself.

You can perform this yoga of self-creation whenever you

need inspiration, whenever you are filled with self-doubt or self-deprecation. You can also do this yoga to focus on specific difficulties you are facing in your personal life or problems that are taking place in the world at large. You can think about places where there is conflict, unhappiness, and confusion, and radiate hope and healing to them. You can visualize people coming to resolution, the earth becoming abundant, the weather becoming beautiful, and all beings becoming happy.

The purpose of this yoga is to provide you with a playful, magical way to experience creative self-confidence. Grounded in the safety net of absolute freedom from a fixed ego, you cultivate a sense of realistic pride and stable self-confidence, not for any selfish purpose but out of altruism, the energy that intensifies your love and benevolence. You are now a true bodhisattva. Universal good emanates from your heroic actions out into the world.

COOL REVOLUTION

What if we had the kind of society in which if we saw someone abusing or harming someone else, we were totally committed to making sure they stopped, as well as to protecting the vulnerable and understanding how the brutality began in the first place? Imagine if our approach to ending violence was determinedly nonviolent. Imagine if instead of rushing to punish and vilify the offender, we paid equal attention to knowing the story of the abuser. That would make it possible to mete out punishment appropriate to the guilty while also addressing the causes and conditions that led to that behavior. What if we directed our animosity toward the crime instead of the criminal? Rather than losing ourselves in personal outrage, what if we directed our outrage toward the systems that help create such disaffected, abandoned, and angry people?

Anger is our default emotion when we're not getting what we want, but the principle of transformative action requires us to think more creatively. We learn that it is possible to respond to grief and fear in ways other than resentment. It is indeed natural to be outraged in the face of injustice or cruelty. But when anger becomes a steady presence, it narrows our perceptions and possibilities.

Remember that anger, like fear, constricts our field of vision. Our practice is to feel outrage when it arises, without allowing it to become our overriding motivation for seeking change. If our goal is to stop a war and end violence, then outrage—no matter how righteous—is not the way to sustain that effort in the long term, with all the uncertainty, hope, grief, and twists and turns we can experience in the process of trying to affect the world.

Ordinarily, we tend to think of pacifism, like kindness and empathy, as a form of weakness. But that misses our need to take a good look at what strength really is. It is possible to be absolutely committed to stopping abuse or injustice and protecting the injured, while tempering outrage with compassion.

My friend Ethan Nichtern, founder of the Interdependence Project, a nonprofit organization dedicated to Buddhist-inspired meditation and mindfulness in psychology, activism, media, and the arts, has written eloquently about why we are often blocked in maintaining this fine balance. If we examine the view of human nature that lies beneath our social niceties, Ethan points out, we find "a fearful sense of what it means to be human." According to the prevailing Western philosophical perspective, put forth most pessimistically by Thomas Hobbes in the 17th century, human beings are naturally inclined to a "war of all against all." Ethan lists "three S's" that, in this view, characterize us above all: Separate, Selfish, and Scared. Dominated by this philosophy, he explains, life becomes "a perpetual battle against the Other, a self-absorbed and fearful fight to protect ourselves and our families against constant threats."[22]

Ethan offers an alternative perspective for a wholly different, more fulfilled, and effective life, defined by three C's: Connection, Compassion, and Courage. He and his colleagues named the shift from the three S's to the three C's "Transformational Activism." It calls for the revisioning of our inner work as individuals, our interpersonal conduct in relationships, and our collective efforts to transform society. In Transformational Activism there is a seamless, reciprocal exchange between our inner life and the expression of our values in the larger world.

All these strategies would nourish our communities and offer lessons for moral and spiritual growth instead of creating more

---

22 See http//www.theidproject.org/.

violence. Albert Einstein said, "The unleashed power of the atom has changed everything save our modes of thinking. . . ."[23] How we think, how we look at our lives, is all-important, and the degree of love we manifest determines the degree of spaciousness and freedom we can bring to life's events. It takes strong insight and a good deal of courage to break away from our habitual ways of looking at things, in order to respond from a different place.

Imagine if we dropped our need to perpetually be seen as right, our easy continuation of what we're used to, and our urge to go along with what others think, and tried to practice the Buddha's teaching that hatred only ceases through love? Shouting to drown out someone else's noise and returning belligerence with belligerence may be automatic, but it tires us out. Rigidly categorizing people as all good or bad or right or wrong helps us feel secure, at least momentarily, but relating in that way doesn't allow us to really connect and leaves us feeling misunderstood and alone. Risking a new way of seeing helps us discover new ways of communicating that convey our feelings honestly without damaging ourselves or those around us.

We are ready for a global shift away from Us-versus-Them animosity—from a world dominated by the notion that "if you're not with me, you're against me, and therefore my enemy" to one of intensified interconnection (growing every day, thanks to the Internet); celebrated diversity; and creative, nonviolent solutions to social and political conflict. It is time to get over the notion that not being lost in enmity is a sign of weakness or giving in. We are ready for another way of viewing strength and a fresh approach to improving life on this planet. Think of Nelson Mandela realizing that his own guards on Robben Island were imprisoned by the system, even as they imprisoned him. Or the Burmese politician Aung San Suu Kyi, who spent 15 years under house arrest for promoting democracy, saying:

---

23 Quoted in "Atomic Education Urged by Einstein," *The New York Times,* May 25, 1946, p. 13, accessed at http://www.nytimes.com.

. . . as time went on, like a lot of others who've been incarcerated, we have discovered the value of lovingkindness. We've found that it's one's own feeling of hostility that generates fear. I never felt frightened when I was surrounded by all those hostile troops. That is because I never felt hostility towards them. As Burmese Buddhists, we put a great emphasis on *metta* (lovingkindness). It's the same idea as in the biblical quotation: "Perfect love casts out fear." While I cannot claim to have discovered "perfect love," I think it's a fact that you are not frightened of people whom you do not hate. Of course, I did get angry occasionally with some of the things they did, but anger as a passing emotion is quite different from the feeling of sustained hatred or hostility.[24]

Or Martin Luther King, Jr., who insisted that we take the long view of justice in dealing with our enemies. "The arc of the moral universe is long, but it bends toward justice," he said.[25]

Such a cool revolution kicks off an enormous adventure of consciousness, a readiness to redefine power and view patience as strength rather than resignation. Even in horrible circumstances, we have the opportunity for meaningful change. I realized this after the bombing of the London Underground in July 2005, when, like most people, my initial response was sorrow for the lives lost and anxiety about getting on a subway back home in New York. While this fear was natural and appropriate, Willa, the seven-year-old daughter of a friend, had another perspective. On being told what had happened in London, her eyes filled with tears and she said, "Mom, we should say a prayer." As she and her mother held hands, Willa asked to go first. Her mother was stunned to hear her daughter begin with, "May the bad guys remember the love in their hearts." Hearing that, my own heart leaped to another level altogether.

---

24   From chapter 10, *Voice of Hope,* by Aung San Suu Kyi and Alan Clements (New York: Seven Stories Press, 1997).

25   From Dr. King's address to the Tenth Anniversary Convention of the Southern Christian Leadership Conference, Atlanta, August 16, 1967.

The much beloved Hindu guru Neem Karoli Baba often said, "Don't throw anyone out of your heart." Some of the most powerful healings—and greatest adventures—of our lifetime can come about as we learn to live by this dictum. Then we will have no qualms about acknowledging our enemies as our greatest teachers. Above all, we'll be able to embrace the world.

Practice Guide: Do This at Home!

It is one thing to read about overcoming our enemies, but how do we actually work on it? What specific practices can we do to transform our relationship with our enemies, inner and outer, and find freedom from anger and fear?

Here are some meditations and visualizations that can help you in applying the teachings on enemies to your own life. Although these techniques are based on Buddhist practices, they are applicable to anyone, regardless of belief system. You will find a practice to deal with each of the four types of enemy—outer, inner, secret, and super-secret—as well as a basic meditation to help you ground yourself in your body, quiet your mind, and open your heart.

Basic Meditation

Sit comfortably, with your back straight. Close your eyes or not, depending on which you prefer. If you feel sleepy, you can open your eyes and gaze softly downward to help you stay awake.

Bring your attention to your body. Be aware of whatever sensations you feel. Notice any sensations in your hands—pulsing, throbbing, pressure. Notice the feeling of your breath at the nostrils or chest or abdomen. Let the breath come and go naturally. Don't try to change or control it. Just feel one breath, and then let it go.

If you wish, you can make a quiet mental note such as *in, out* or *rising, falling* to support the feeling of the breath. But let your awareness rest primarily on the sensations themselves, not on the words that accompany them.

As images and emotions arise in your mind, as you become aware of sounds around you, don't dwell on them. Simply notice them, and then let them pass. Stay connected to the feeling of the breath. If an image or sensation becomes strong enough to grab your attention, or you find yourself lost in thought, or you start to fall asleep, gently bring your awareness back to the breath.

Working with the Outer Enemy

Think of someone you don't like, someone you feel real antipathy toward. It may be someone you find frightening, someone you find challenging, someone you see as a rival, or someone who has harmed you in some way. Bring the person clearly to mind and visualize them sitting before you. Really get in touch with your feelings toward that person. Feel the anger or fear or distaste as it arises in you.

Now put yourself in the other person's shoes. Imagine being that person, sitting there looking at you. See yourself from your enemy's perspective. Realize that your enemy is mirroring your feelings toward them. Just as you see your enemy, your enemy sees you the same way. Perhaps you are jealous of them, if they seem to be one-up and looking down at you. Or you may feel superior and therefore have a condescending attitude toward the enemy. Look at yourself through eyes of jealousy, envy, competitiveness, and condescension.

When you have thoroughly immersed yourself in the negative feelings you have for your enemy and your enemy has for you, realize that you don't have to harbor those feelings. You can see your enemy in a different way. Try to imagine how their loved ones see them, how their child sees them, or how their pet dog sees them. If your enemy seems particularly bad, imagine how their partner in crime sees them—as an ally, a co-conspirator, a friend. And then note how stressed your enemy feels on seeing or thinking of you. It is the same stress that you feel when you see or think of your enemy.

As you look at yourself through this other person's eyes, note the tone of voice you are using in your mind. Be aware of how your condescension, competitiveness, contempt, or jealousy is conveyed in the little things you do and say. Your emotions emerge in your voice and speech and gestures and body language, just as your enemy's emotions are written all over their face and behavior.

Now try to see something beautiful in your enemy. Imagine that person being really happy at having fallen in love or won an election or won the lottery. (If you're really daring, imagine your enemy winning the battle with you. That should make your enemy feel good!) Imagine your enemy being happy to see you, or if you can't quite summon up that vision, imagine them at least as not being angry with you. Imagine your enemy being happy enough with their own life to have neither the time nor the inclination to bother you. Think of what would make your enemy truly satisfied, truly pleased. It may not be what you assume your enemy wants—that is, domination over you. When you are no longer bothering your enemy, no longer standing in the way of what that person wants, then your enemy will no longer be interested in bothering you.

In visualizing yourself from the enemy's perspective, you start to see that what makes you vulnerable to your enemies is your sense of being fundamentally different from them. But when you realize that in very basic ways you are the same—at a minimum, you share a desire to be happy and not to be in pain—then you don't want to spoil the happiness of your enemies any more than you want them to spoil yours.

When you truly grasp that it is the projection of your own hurt and anger and fear that turns someone into your enemy, and you are able to recognize your kinship as fellow human beings, it releases the energy you previously invested in defending yourself and your ego. Now you can use this precious energy to work on rooting out the inner enemies, such as anger, fear, and jealousy. In this way, the enemy you so disliked becomes your ally: your teacher, your helper, even—dare I say it—your friend.

Eventually you will even be able to see the beauty in your enemy, and you will feel free of inner anxiety about them. Then, whenever you happen to meet that person, you will notice that they seem less troublesome to you. And your new attitude toward your former enemy will affect them, too, and they will be less antagonistic toward you, though they may not consciously know why.

Now you can meditate on seeing your life as one of being among friends.

WORKING WITH THE INNER ENEMY

LOVINGKINDNESS

Lovingkindness, with the wish for all beings to be happy, is a classical Buddhist teaching that is held within the group of four qualities called the *brahma-viharas*—"boundless states," or "supreme abidings." (The other three qualities are compassion, sympathetic joy, and equanimity.) As a practice, lovingkindness is based on a sense of friendship and inclusivity, of kinship with others.

In this meditation, we gather our attention through the silent repetition of certain basic phrases that are the expression of our heart's energy. We make this offering of happiness and well-being first to ourselves, and then we gradually widen our field of attention to all beings everywhere. You do not have to be sitting in formal meditation to practice lovingkindness. It is a practice you can ultimately take with you anywhere—walking down the street, sitting on the bus, waiting for a doctor's appointment.

If you are doing a formal meditation practice, begin by sitting comfortably. Close your eyes or not—whichever you prefer. See if three or four phrases come to mind that you would like to repeat as a blessing to yourself and others. Or you can repeat the classical phrases:

> **May I be happy.**
> **May I be healthy.**
> **May I be safe.**
> **May I live with ease.**

(The last phrase is not a wish for luxury, but rather that your livelihood and relationships and other aspects of daily life not be a struggle.)

Silently repeat these phrases for a few minutes. Then think of a benefactor—someone who has been good to you, who has been generous to you, who has helped you in some way. The Buddhist texts say that the benefactor is a person who, when you think of them, makes you smile. Bring to mind an image of that person and get a feeling of their importance in your life. Then offer them the phrases:

> **May you be happy.**
> **May you be healthy.**
> **May you be safe.**
> **May you live with ease.**

Next, think of a friend who is doing pretty well right now. The person might not be perfectly happy but is basically feeling pretty good, and their life seems to be working well. Bring this person to mind and offer them the phrases of lovingkindness.

And now think of a friend who is not doing so well, who is suffering in some way. Offer that friend the phrases of lovingkindness.

Next, think of someone toward whom you have neutral feelings. Maybe an acquaintance or someone you don't even know by name. It might be the newsstand proprietor from whom you buy your morning paper, or the UPS driver who brings parcels to your office, or someone on the treadmill next to you at the gym. Offer the phrases of lovingkindness to this person.

Now think of someone you have some difficulty with. It's usually not recommended to start with the person who has hurt or betrayed you the most, or someone on the world stage who has behaved so terribly that it seems inconceivable to include them in this practice. Start with someone with whom you have had a minor conflict or toward whom you have some feelings of unease. Bring this person to mind and see what happens as you repeat the phrases of lovingkindness for them.

And finally, offer the phrases of lovingkindness to all beings everywhere—people, animals, all creatures. *May all beings be happy, healthy, and safe, and live with ease.*

The first few times you practice lovingkindness, you may find it difficult to offer it to your enemy, even to a mildly difficult person. Perhaps you will want to skip your enemy and go on to all beings, or return to offering lovingkindness to yourself. That's perfectly all right. Over time, as you continue to do the practice including everyone, everywhere, you will find yourself experiencing a sense of kinship with all beings that begins to break down any barriers you have erected between yourself and others. It becomes easier and easier to include even your designated enemies in the vast circle of connection.

COMPASSION

Compassion enables a movement toward a painful situation to see if we can be of help. Practicing compassion counteracts cruelty. It also enables us to face our own or others' pain without being overwhelmed. It is a movement of the heart, not a sentiment. Compassion has qualities of self-sufficiency, of wholeness, of resiliency. It is born out of truly knowing our oneness with others, not just thinking about it or wishing it were so.

The stability of compassion arises from steering clear of a shallow martyrdom in which we think only of others and never care about ourselves. Conversely, we also relinquish the ordinary kind of self-caring in which we think only about ourselves and don't consider others.

The meditation to cultivate compassion is similar to the lovingkindness meditation, though often the phrases used are something like *May you be free of pain and sorrow* and *May you be well and happy*. Remember that the phrases are meant to serve as the conduit for the heart's energy, so the words need not be perfect. In certain situations, such as when someone is suffering a grave illness, you may want to adapt the phrases to the circumstances.

The sequence of the compassion meditation is also somewhat altered from that of the lovingkindness meditation in that we begin with someone we know who is in difficulty. This should be a real person, not a composite you dream up to stand in for a category of sufferers—all homeless people, say. After a few minutes of offering compassion to this person, move on through the sequence of the lovingkindness meditation.

Before you begin the compassion meditation, you can reflect on our shared vulnerability as human beings. It's not that we all have the same burden of pain by any means, but we do all share in the uncertainty and insecurity of existence. With one phone call, your entire life can change. This understanding should bring us closer to one another and make us more caring. The sense of oneness and connection is, in itself, uplifting.

SYMPATHETIC JOY

Sympathetic joy is genuine delight in the happiness of others—feeling pleasure at their good fortune rather than thinking, *Ewww, I wish things weren't going so well for you.* An antidote to envy and resentment, sympathetic joy is a beautiful quality but one that is not easy to summon up, because of our ambivalent feelings about others' success, especially when we think the prize they won should have been ours. Other people's good fortune raises fears that there is only so much happiness to go around and therefore we cannot all be winners. Sympathetic joy brings us face to face with deep-seated feelings about competition and scarcity—inner enemies that fuel the creation of outer enemies.

The practice of sympathetic joy opens us to the reality of all that we *do* have, counterbalancing our feelings of scarcity and failure, and our resentment toward anyone we see as more fortunate than us.

The meditation on sympathetic joy is similar to the lovingkindness meditation, although the phrases often used are something like *May your happiness and good fortune not diminish* and *May they increase further and further.*

We start the sequence of sympathetic joy with a friend who is relatively happy right now. They might not be perfectly happy, but they are enjoying success or good fortune in at least some area of life. And we skip ourselves, since by definition sympathetic joy is happiness for the happiness of others.

In lieu of including ourselves, before we begin the sequence of phrases, we reflect on the goodness in our own lives. Since one of the hindrances to sympathetic joy is a feeling of lack, we take the time to consider what we can appreciate and be grateful for. This reflection all by itself is a powerful antidote to the inner enemies of craving and frustration.

EQUANIMITY

Equanimity, or balance of mind, is in many ways the foundation of the other three boundless states. It is the unspoken wisdom that allows us to broaden our caring beyond our own inner circle, making the practices of lovingkindness, compassion, and sympathetic joy true expressions of a generous spirit.

Without equanimity, we might offer friendship only when our offering was acknowledged and appreciated, or only when the person responded in kind. We might offer compassion to ourselves only when we weren't overcome by pain, and offer compassion to others only when we weren't overcome by their suffering. And we might offer sympathetic joy only when we did not feel threatened or envious. When we cultivate equanimity, our tremendous capacity to connect with others can blossom, for we don't feel the need to reject or cling to anything that happens in life.

The foundation of equanimity is reflecting on what are called, in Buddhist teachings, the eight vicissitudes, or eight worldly conditions: pleasure and pain, gain and loss, praise and blame, and fame and disrepute—the inevitable ups and downs of life. The eight vicissitudes make up the very fabric of life, true for us all, not just for some. Recognizing and accepting this reality provides the largest possible context for developing lovingkindness, compassion, and sympathetic joy.

In equanimity practice we begin by repeating the phrases with a neutral person in mind, then a benefactor, and so on through the sequence, finally ending with ourselves. Possible phrases would be: *Things are as they are. I care about you, yet I can't control how your life will evolve. All beings are the owners of their actions; their happiness and unhappiness depend upon their actions, not upon my wishes for them.*

Working with the Secret Enemy

GIVE AND TAKE

Transforming our relationship with people we perceive as enemies involves the daily practice of exchanging self-preoccupation for other-preoccupation. To assist us in this, as a kind of rehearsal for the altruistic behavior where we actually take others' suffering upon ourselves, we have the special meditation of give and take, in which we imagine that we give our happiness to others and take on their suffering.

> Hold your enemy's image in your mind, or picture your enemy sitting in front of you. As you breathe out, share all your happiness, all your light, with your enemy. Let your enemy have a feeling of connection to your shining mind.
>
> Then, as you breathe in, take the irritation, the anger, and the rage, from your enemy and draw that energy into yourself. Whatever hostility they feel for you, invite that in. And then let that force direct itself toward your inner enemy, overcoming your inner enemy without harming your shining mind. Now your outer enemy is working for you without realizing it, helping you free yourself from your inner enemy, your habitual reactive self that is continually absorbed with *me-me-me, I like this, I want more*. You turn the enemy's energy into positive energy, which you experience as a feeling of relief and peace.
>
> Now, as you breathe out, the light of your shining mind flows out to your enemy, reinforced by the blessings of your protectors—whether it's Jesus, Mary, Abraham, Muhammad, the Buddha, Kuan Yin, the Dalai Lama, a saint or angel, your guru, or whoever it may be. As you continue to breathe in and out, you can silently repeat to yourself the following:

[Inhale] Destroy my inner enemy, my egotism.
[Exhale] Share my love, my wisdom.
[Inhale] Destroy my inner enemy, my egotism, my
    attachment, my aversion.
[Exhale] Share my love, my happiness, my blessing.

Continue going back and forth, taking in the enemy's hostility and giving it to your egotism as you inhale, and then, as you exhale, giving happiness to your enemy from your liberated, loving ego.

As you practice give and take with your enemy, your egotistical, self-preoccupied persona becomes more and more subdued; and your altruistic, loving, happy self emerges. Your self-cherishing, self-aggrandizing, discontented, angry self becomes increasingly weaker, while your enlightened self grows stronger. Loving your enemy in this way is enlightened self-interest: you gain strength from your altruism. And the blessings spread far and wide—to your loved ones, to neutral ones, to all beings. When you can give to your enemy even the slightest bit, you become an artist of your own life.

Working with the Super-secret Enemy

EXCHANGE OF SELF AND OTHER

Our outer enemies are our greatest teachers, directing us toward the real enemy, our self-preoccupation. In the practice of exchanging self-preoccupation for other-preoccupation, we expand our identity to embrace all other beings, moving from egotism and self-obsession to altruism and compassion.

Begin by turning your mindful awareness back upon yourself, looking into your own face, as it were. When you do, you see through yourself, in that you scan within and cannot find a fixed identity anywhere—not in your face, your brain, your heart. Let yourself melt into the clear light of the void plenum of infinite energy. Do not be afraid of this energy: it only envelops everything as infinite potential. Yet you can draw upon it inexhaustibly with your love—your will to happiness for yourself and others. In that sense the clear light of the void of ultimate reality is nothing but pure love: infinite abundant energy to satisfy all needs of all beings, never overwhelming but always responsive to every need.

Now draw upon this infinite energy to imagine yourself manifesting whatever it is that you and all those you love really need. Imagine your body as possessing whatever capability is useful, and imagine your mind as tirelessly and joyfully creative in providing whatever others need. Feel real happiness as the natural condition of every cell within you and every energy around you. Remember that you are not a fixed, hard structure, but a vibrant field of quantum energy, healed within and capable of healing everyone and everything around you. Imagine all beings looking at you and seeing you radiating liquid light—jewellike rays of diamond, topaz, ruby, emerald, and sapphire, edged with gold and silver sparkles.

Enjoy this visualization for as long as you like, remembering that this is the reality we do not normally see because of our habit of concretizing our perceptions of material things. Dedicate the pleasure and merit of your visualization to becoming a being that can always feel and emanate in this way. Realize that every being has the exact same ultimate reality and relative potential, and so resolve never to put yourself forward as special. Restrain any desire to be especially honored or praised by others, and instead realize that your blissfulness is what makes you competent to serve others. Then, as you go on about your daily activities, do not be tempted to hold yourself apart from others or above them in any way.

ABOUT THE AUTHOR

 **Sharon Salzberg**, a teacher of meditation for more than 30 years, co-founded the Insight Meditation Society in Barre, Massachusetts, the Forest Refuge and the Barre Center for Buddhist Studies. Sharon's work is based on the practices of mindfulness and *metta*, (lovingkindness), the aim of which is to cultivate love and compassion both for ourselves and for others. 'This,' she explains, 'is the heart of the Buddha's teaching: in each of us is a genuine capacity for love, forgiveness, wisdom and compassion, and by practising meditation these qualities are brought to life. Any of us can discover for ourselves the unique happiness that is our birthright.'

Her books include *Lovingkindness, Faith, The Force of Kindness* and the *New York Times* bestseller *Real Happiness* (published in the UK as *The Power of Meditation*). She blogs for *The Huffington Post;* has been a contributing editor at *O, the Oprah Magazine;* and has been featured in periodicals such as *Time, Real Simple, Good Housekeeping, Self, Tricycle: The Buddhist Review* and the *Shambhala Sun.*

www.sharonsalzberg.com

ABOUT THE AUTHOR

 **Tenzin Robert Thurman** is the Jey Tsong Khapa Professor of Indo-Tibetan Buddhist Studies at Columbia University, holding the first endowed chair of Buddhist Studies in the United States. He is the author of the bestseller *Inner Revolution*, as well as *Anger*, *Infinite Life* and other popular books. He is also a translator of Tibetan texts. The first Westerner ordained as a Buddhist mendicant by His Holiness the Dalai Lama, Thurman later returned to lay life, keeping the ordination name 'Tenzin' as a nickname. A close friend of His Holiness over the last 48 years, he serves as co-founder and president of Tibet House US, a non-profit organization dedicated to preserving the endangered culture of Tibet. As the director of the Tengyur Translation Initiative, he oversees, at His Holiness's request, the translation of major Tibetan-language Buddhist arts and sciences texts from the library of the ancient Nalanda University of Buddhist India.

www.bobthurman.com

Hay House Titles of Related Interest

YOU CAN HEAL YOUR LIFE, the movie,
starring Louise L. Hay & Friends
(available as a 1-DVD programme and an expanded 2-DVD set)
Watch the trailer at: **www.LouiseHayMovie.com**

THE SHIFT, the movie,
starring Dr Wayne W. Dyer
(available as a 1-DVD programme and an expanded 2-DVD set)
Watch the trailer at: **www.DyerMovie.com**

*AWAKENING THE LUMINOUS MIND: Tibetan Meditation
for Inner Peace and Joy,* by Tenzin Wangyal Rinpoche

*FEEDING YOUR DEMONS: Ancient Wisdom for
Resolving Inner Conflict,* by Tsultrim Allione

*THE MINDFUL MANIFESTO: How doing less and
noticing more can help us thrive in a stressed-out world,*
by Dr Jonty Heaversedge & Ed Halliwell

*ONE-MINUTE MINDFULNESS: How to Live
in the Moment,* by Simon Parke

All of the above are available at your local bookstore,
or may be ordered by contacting Hay House (see next page).

We hope you enjoyed this Hay House book. If you'd like to receive our online catalogue featuring additional information on Hay House books and products, or if you'd like to find out more about the Hay Foundation, please contact:

Hay House UK, Ltd.,
Astley House, 33 Notting Hill Gate, London W11 3JQ
Phone: 0-20-3675-2450 • *Fax:* 0-20-3675-2451
www.hayhouse.co.uk • www.hayfoundation.org

Published and distributed in the United States by: Hay House, Inc., P.O. Box 5100, Carlsbad, CA 92018-5100
Phone: (760) 431-7695 or (800) 654-5126
Fax: (760) 431-6948 or (800) 650-5115
www.hayhouse.com®

Published and distributed in Australia by: Hay House Australia Pty. Ltd., 18/36 Ralph St., Alexandria NSW 2015 • *Phone:* 612-9669-4299
Fax: 612-9669-4144 • www.hayhouse.com.au

Published and distributed in the Republic of South Africa by: Hay House SA (Pty), Ltd., P.O. Box 990, Witkoppen 2068 • *Phone/Fax:* 27-11-467-8904
www.hayhouse.co.za

Published in India by: Hay House Publishers India, Muskaan Complex, Plot No. 3, B-2, Vasant Kunj, New Delhi 110 070 • *Phone:* 91-11-4176-1620
Fax: 91-11-4176-1630 • www.hayhouse.co.in

Distributed in Canada by: Raincoast, 9050 Shaughnessy St., Vancouver, B.C. V6P 6E5 • *Phone:* (604) 323-7100 • *Fax:* (604) 323-2600
www.raincoast.com

Take Your Soul on a Vacation

Visit **www.HealYourLife.com**® to regroup, recharge, and reconnect with your own magnificence.

Featuring blogs, mind-body-spirit news, and life-changing wisdom from Louise Hay and friends.

Visit **www.HealYourLife.com** today!